A note on the author:

Gerald M. Berkowitz is Professor of English at Northern Illinois University. He is also the author of *David Garrick: A Reference Guide* and *Sir John Vanburgh and the End of the Restoration Comedy*. He has the distinction of being the world's "most ardent theatregoer" in the Guiness World Book of Records for having once attended 145 plays in 25 days.

New Broadways

New Broadways

THEATRE ACROSS AMERICA 1950-1980

Gerald M. Berkowitz

ROWMAN & ALLANHELD
Totowa, New Jersey

To My Parents

ROWMAN & ALLANHELD PUBLISHERS

Copyright © 1982 by Rowman and Littlefield

All rights reserved. No part of this publication may be
reproduced or transmitted, in any form or by any means, without the
permission of the Publishers.

First published in the United States 1982 by Rowman and Littlefield,
81 Adams Drive, Totowa, New Jersey 07512.

Library of Congress Cataloging in Publication Data

Berkowitz, Gerald M.
  New Broadways.

  Includes bibliographical references and
index.
  1. Theater—United States—History—20th
century. I. Title.
PN2266.B49   792'.0973   81-21162
ISBN 0-8476-7031-7   AACR2

83 84 85 86 87 10 9 8 7 6 5 4 3 2

Printed in the United States of America

Contents

Illustrations   vi
Preface   viii

1   Prologue: The American Theatre in 1950   1
2   Off-Broadway   23
3   Regional Theatre   55
4   Off Off and Other Alternatives   95
5   Broadway   143
6   Epilogue: The American Theatre in 1980   175

Index   186

Illustrations

Times Square.   Frontispiece
Williams's *A Streetcar Named Desire:* Marlon Brando,
    Jessica Tandy.   8
Rodgers's and Hammerstein's *South Pacific:* Ezio Pinza,
    Mary Martin.   14
Elia Kazan.   18
José Quintero.   28
Eugene O'Neill.   30
O'Neill's *Long Day's Journey into Night:* Florence Eldridge,
    Bradford Dillman, Jason Robards Jr., Frederick March. 32
The Living Theatre 1961. Jack Gelber, Julian Beck,
    Judith Malina, Merce Cunningham, Peter Feldman,
    James Spicer.   34
The Phoenix Theatre: T. Edward Hambleton, Norris
    Houghton, Jerome Robbins.   36
Joseph Papp.   38
Albee's *Who's Afraid of Virginia Woolf?* Margo Skinner,
    Richard Kneeland.   44
Lowell's *The Old Glory:* Frank Langella, Roscoe Lee
    Browne.   47
Delacorte Theater, Central Park.   50
Margo Jones.   57
Nina Vance.   59
Zelda Fichandler.   60

Tyrone Guthrie.   62
Rostand's *Cyrano de Bergerac:* William Ball, Paul Shenar.   64
Gordon Davidson.   67
The Music Center of the County of Los Angeles.   68
The Mark Taper Forum.   69
Lincoln Center.   71
Vivian Beaumont Theater.   72
Albee's *Box-Mao-Box:* Lucille Patton, Conrad Yama,
    William Needles, Jenny Egan.   81
Coburn's *The Gin Game:* Jessica Tandy, Hume Cronyn.   82
Sackler's *The Great White Hope:* James Earl Jones.   84
Alley Theatre, Houston.   85
Joe Cino.   96
Ellen Stewart.   101
Freeman's *Jesse and the Bandit Queen:* Bryan Clark, Jill
    Eikenberry.   106
San Francisco Mime Troupe: *False Promises.*   107
The Living Theatre: *Paradise Now.*   110
Tom O'Horgan.   117
O'Horgan's *Hair.*   118
Marshall W. Mason.   122
Sam Shepard.   128
Shepard's *The Tooth of Crime:* Ed Hall, James
    Eichelberger, Bruce McGill.   130
Shepard's *Buried Child.*   132
Lanford Wilson.   133
Wilson's *The Hot l Baltimore:* Zane Lansky, Conchata
    Ferrell.   134
Wilson's *Fifth of July:* Joyce Reehling, Jonathan Hogan.   135
Mamet's *A Life in the Theatre:* Michael Nussbaum,
    Cosmo White.   137
Rabe's *Streamers.*   139
Tennessee Williams.   145
Arthur Miller.   150
Sondheim's *A Chorus Line.*   162
Sondheim's *Company:* Larry Kert and cast.   164
Harold Prince and Stephen Sondheim.   166
TKTS Booth, Duffy Square.   170
Medoff's *Children of a Lesser God:* Phyllis Frelich, John
    Rubinstein.   178
Cristofer's *The Shadow Box:* David Huffman, Laurence
    Luckinbill, Cynthia Harris.   182

Preface

This is the account of thirty years in the history of the professional American theatre. They were a very significant thirty years and this history, unlike many, has a plot—one of growth and change and liberation. If it doesn't have a happy ending, that's because the story isn't over; certainly things are happier when it stops than they were when it began.

The third quarter of the twentieth century saw two overwhelming changes in the fate of the American theatre, its expansion to truly national proportions and its evolution from a purely commercial enterprise to, in many cases, an institutional status approaching those of museums and symphony orchestras. As is not always the case with such expansion and evolution, the process was not accompanied by a decline in creativity or vitality; on almost every possible scale the American theatre was healthier, more creative and more appreciated in 1980 than in 1950. How, why, and with whom that happened is the subject of this book.

Any general survey must be selective, and my mode has been to focus on outstanding or representative illustrations of each development or stage in the history of the theatre since 1950. To those whom I have omitted, and particularly to those whom I may inadvertently have misrepresented in attempting to fit them into the general picture, my apologies. To those readers looking for details and insights beyond the scope of this study I recommend all of the volumes listed in the notes to each chapter, and three resources in particular. The first is the *New York Times,* whose reporting, analysis and commentary on the theatre, particularly in its Sunday Arts section, is unmatched; virtually all the uncredited facts and statistics in this study came from its pages. Second is the *Best Plays* series published annually by Dodd, Mead & Company and edited during the period covered by this history by John Chapman, Louis Kronenberger, Henry Hewes and Otis L. Guernsey, Jr. in turn; in addition to selections from the best plays each season these volumes offer descriptions and complete production data for all Broadway shows and, increasingly through the years, for Off-Broadway, Off Off-Broadway and regional productions as well. As a convenient source of raw data and of clear and frequently entertaining summaries of theatrical news, these volumes cannot be bettered. The final resource is not a book but a repository: the Billy Rose Theatre Collection of the New York Public Library, whose seemingly endless supply of theatrical records, clippings, programs, photographs and manuscripts is enough to frighten one away from a project like this, and enough to enable one to undertake it.

I must thank the writers of all the books I used, the journalists of the *Times,* the *Best Plays* editors, and the contributors to and staff of the Theatre Collection; not only did they make the writing of this book possible, but they made it exciting. I thank Northern Illinois University for granting me a year's leave and further released time for research and writing. Jim Feather of Rowman and Littlefield was the ideal taskmaster, knowing exactly when to give me my head and when to crack the whip. And Alfred Weiss, my uncle, colleague and friend, who has shared his love of theatre with me all my life, shared his knowledge and editorial skills just as unselfishly while I worked on this project. The book would be dedicated to him were there not two people with a prior claim.

Times Square.
(Courtesy of the New York Convention & Visitors Bureau)

CHAPTER 1

Prologue:
The American Theatre
in 1950

The city of New York has five subdivisions called boroughs, of which the most famous is Manhattan, an island near the mouth of the Hudson River, about fourteen miles long and two miles across. Except for the southern tip, which is old New Amsterdam and has the winding streets of a European city, Manhattan is laid out on a grid, with numbered streets going east and west, and numbered avenues north and south. The notable exception is Broadway, which cuts across the grid on a rough diagonal from southeast to northwest. Broadway crosses Seventh Avenue at Forty-fifth Street, and the lopsided-hourglass-shaped plaza thus formed, extending from Forty-third to Forty-seventh, is Times Square. On the streets off Times Square are about thirty theatres, most built in the first quarter of the twentieth century, with conventional proscenium stages and an average capacity of about 1200.

And that, in 1950, was the American theatre.

That is an oversimplification, of course, but not a misleading one. With some significant exceptions, theatre outside New York—indeed, outside that square mile of Manhattan—consisted essentially of amateur and student groups, road companies and summer stock revivals of Broadway hits and, in a narrow corridor of northeastern cities, pre-Broadway tryouts. The vital center of the American theatre, the source of its dramatic literature and its acting and production styles, and the home (or goal) of its most talented actors, directors, composers and designers was Broadway.

It had not always been thus. Indeed, this extreme centralization was a fairly recent development in the history of a broadly national American theatre. The first recorded performance of European-style theatre on the American continent was in the Spanish Southwest in 1598, and there were flourishing theatres throughout the British colonies from the early eighteenth century. Through most of the Colonial period and well into the nineteenth century Philadelphia was the theatrical capital, with major companies and active theatres in Williamsburg, Charleston, Annapolis, Boston, Baltimore and Washington as well as New York, while secondary companies operated in or regularly visited New Orleans, Cincinnati, Pittsburgh and almost every other big or medium-sized city. The expansion of the country brought an expansion of the American theatre, with the "opera house" ranking just behind the schoolhouse, church, jail and saloon as a construction priority in every new western town with any pretension to culture. Although the center shifted from Philadelphia to New York, by the middle of the nineteenth century every large city and many smaller ones had resident professional stock companies; and new plays were as likely to be produced in, say, Chicago or St. Louis as in New York. Big stars, British and American, could tour the entire country, performing with local companies which had rehearsed around them. As late as 1900 there were about two thousand such companies across the continent, with repertoires that included classics and new works as well as New York successes and touring shows.

No single event caused the collapse of all these theatres, but the growing importance of New York as a producing center was a major factor; New York–based entrepreneurs discovered that it cost very little more to send a complete cast on tour than just one or two stars, and that local companies deprived of their guest stars posed little competition. As the practice of repertory booking—that is, a different play each night—gradually gave way in the nineteenth century to long runs of single plays, the phenomenon of the Broadway hit was created, and plays bearing the glory of New York success became more attractive to regional audiences than locally produced new works. In 1896 the biggest New York and Philadelphia producers formed a play-producing, tour-booking and theatre-owning cartel commonly called the Syndicate, and the remaining independent local companies and producers began to fall by the wayside. The advent of movies struck the final blow to the local stock companies, as it did to that other immensely vital and national art form, vaudeville. By 1920 at the latest, American theatre meant New York theatre, and New York theatre meant Broadway.

That this situation was inherently harmful to the theatre is obvious. Unlike the similar centralization of the motion picture industry in Hollywood, the Broadway monopoly severely limited the opportunity for audiences around the country to see first-class theatrical productions. A film could play simultaneously in hundreds of theatres, with every audience getting the same quality entertainment. But when even major cities such as Chicago and Los Angeles had to rely on the brief visits of New York–based road companies and the modest offerings of local groups that might be only a short step above amateur status, the experience of seeing the best theatre America had to offer at midcentury was limited to those lucky enough to live in or visit New York City.

And the theatre itself suffered. Talented and ambitious actors, directors and designers were drawn to Broadway, where the inevitably fierce competition meant that many would never get their chance; and there was no alternative arena, particularly for those wishing to do experimental or innovative work. The odds were even worse for young dramatists, since Broadway was the source of virtually all the new plays produced in the country. (I must repeat my *caveat* that the situation was not as absolutely bleak as these generalizations suggest, but the few exceptions did not significantly affect the overall picture.)

On the other hand, the concentration of theatrical activity in New York for more than three decades had some salutory effects. It allowed the twentieth-century American theatre and drama to develop a unity and identity that could not otherwise

3

have appeared. By choice, inertia, inbreeding or historical accident there was in 1950 a distinctly American style in drama, acting and production.

The eighteenth and nineteenth centuries were fallow periods for dramatic literature throughout the world, and the serious American drama was really born in the early twentieth century with the plays of James A. Herne, Edward Sheldon and, above all, Eugene O'Neill. The rapid growth of its early years allowed for some diversity of styles and forms, from O'Neill's experiments in expressionism and epic drama through Maxwell Anderson's verse plays and Thornton Wilder's testing of the limits of stage space and time. But though experiments continued, the American drama found its true voice in the 1930s and 1940s in realistic domestic contemporary middle-class melodrama—that is, in plays that showed the important issues of life reflected and expressed in the personal lives of ordinary people. After trying virtually every imaginable dramatic style, Eugene O'Neill returned in his great final masterpieces to the domestic setting and realistic mode, finding metaphors for his deepest metaphysical explorations in family quarrels and barroom dreams. During the 1930s social critics such as Clifford Odets and Sidney Kingsley expressed their analyses of economic and political forces by dramatizing their effect on the day-to-day lives of ordinary people. And two writers who appeared in the 1940s dominated and defined the serious American drama at midcentury.

Arthur Miller (b. 1915) and Tennessee Williams (b. 1911), despite radically different backgrounds, had strikingly parallel early careers. Both were of the generation that came of age in the Depression, an experience that shook the security of their middle-class families. Both began writing in college, experimenting with fiction and poetry as well as drama. After a false start—Miller's first Broadway play closed after four performances and Williams's died in its pre-Broadway tryout—each entered the scene with an award-winning play and followed up with a truly major work, unquestionably the best play of his entire career. And though both toyed with elements of expressionism, their plays were rooted in the tradition of realistic domestic melodrama.

The differences between the two mark the bounds of the mainstream American drama of midcentury. Miller was the

4

artistic heir of Ibsen and, more directly, of Odets and the socialist writers of the 1930s; he shared with them the impulse toward social criticism and the need to write plays that were overtly About Something, with his characters clearly representatives of larger forces or issues. But, as Harold Clurman notes, "while many dramatists of that period were bent on recording the shock of opposing forces—capital and labor, democracy and fascism, etc.—Miller examines the individual in his moral behavior under specific social pressures."[1] His criticism was always personal and specific, not theoretical; his subject was the manner in which individual crises and tragedies pointed up injustices in the state, the society or even the universe.

Miller's first success, *All My Sons* (1947), addresses the issue of public morality vs. private morality, the same question that animates most of Shakespeare's tragedies and histories. But Miller's hero is an ordinary, middle-class American, and his dilemma is presented in recognizable terms. A munitions manufacturer, he has allowed a shipment of defective airplane parts to leave the factory because to do otherwise would be to fail in what he has been taught is his primary moral obligation—to provide for his family. The events of the play force him to recognize that larger social obligations should have taken precedence and that his sense of family should have extended to include the fliers who would be killed in his planes. If the larger themes of *All My Sons* are sometimes awkwardly grafted onto the personal domestic situation (the actual plot centering on the desire of the manufacturer's son to marry the daughter of a man his father ruined), the play illustrates the three assumptions that were to characterize Miller's work: that the values or roles taught by society can be actively harmful in practice, that large moral issues are reflected in the lives of ordinary people, and that therefore the Common Man (Miller's phrase) can be shown dramatically to experience crises of heroic and even tragic proportions.

Death of a Salesman (1949), considered by many to be the archetypal American play, is written in the same mold. Its plot is deceptively ordinary: Willy Loman, an aging salesman, loses his job and, he believes, the respect of his family. Unable to bear the sense of failure, he kills himself in the hope that his insurance money will help his sons to succeed. But Miller shows us that Willy's failure is a failure of the system. The

American Dream that promised success and happiness to the hard worker simply does not deliver, and Willy's tragedy is not that he has failed, but that he has been failed. The system has cheated him while simultaneously controlling his perceptions, so that his only explanation for his failure is that he wasn't good enough. Meanwhile his elder son makes the conceptual leap to the realization that true success lies in self-fulfillment, which can be found even in economic failure. The play is thus About Something—the failure and dishonesty of the American Dream—but is expressed almost entirely through the domestic situation, the relations between Willy and his family and neighbors. Again Miller makes three central statements: while arguing his broader social point and demonstrating its applicability to a specific case, he also celebrates the majesty of the Common Man by showing that the largest issues and emotions are within the scope of his experience.

If Miller belonged to a dramatic school extending at least as far back as Ibsen, Tennessee Williams had less in common with any previous playwrights than with that school of southern gothic novelists that found in extreme and even bizarre circumstances some insights into the mysteries of ordinary human emotions. The son of a minister's daughter and a traveling salesman, he embodied the passionate contradictions of the southern sensibility, along with a poet's mastery of language and love of symbols, and a homosexual's empathy for social outcasts. That last element is the one that most critics and audiences have seen as (to use Clurman's words) "the essential trait of his work: identification with and compassion for victims of our society—the outsider, the shamed, the forsaken, the condemned, the ostracized. . . . He doubts that they will ever achieve a state of grace [but] there is the abiding hope of understanding and consequently forgiveness."[2] Thus, while Miller's attention was drawn outward to social issues, Williams looked inward to understand the psychological and emotional burdens of his characters. And while Miller celebrated the unappreciated nobility of the common man, Williams sought to expand our definition of humanity by showing how much we shared with the cripples and freaks of the world.

Williams's first success, *The Glass Menagerie* (1944), is the story of an emotionally crippled family inhabiting a private world set in but apart from the realities of Depression America.

The mother is a former Southern belle constantly hiding from the present in memories of the past; the daughter is a cripple unable to cope with the outside world; the son is a would-be poet straining to escape both the sterility of the home and the responsibility of a factory job. Mother forces son to bring a fellow worker home as a gentleman caller for the daughter, but the young man is already engaged, foiling her hopes. The play is really about the beautiful fragility of these characters, symbolized by the daughter's collection of glass animals, and the understanding that they are safer in their dreams than in the real world to which the son finally escapes, only to be haunted by his ties to the haven he left behind.

Eugene O'Neill's *Long Day's Journey into Night* is probably the greatest play ever written by an American, but if it isn't, then Williams's *A Streetcar Named Desire* (1947) is. Far more violent and passion-filled than the elegiac *Glass Menagerie*, it provides two of the most vibrant characters (and challenging acting roles) in all of world drama. Blanche Dubois, a faded beauty whose sense of culture has repressed and perverted her capacity for passion, is matched against the crude but unquenchably vital Stanley Kowalski in a battle that achieves mythic scope, the confrontation of a beautiful and noble but enervated civilization and the raw energy of the survival instinct. But the focus is on the individuals, not the mythic forces behind them, and the play is about frightened people fighting to survive. It is a mark of Williams's courage and honesty that although his sympathies are obviously with Blanche, he not only accepts Stanley's inevitable victory but justifies it by showing that Blanche's culture is ultimately life-denying and Stanley's sexual energy is supportive. In the frightening world Williams sees, anything that enables man to survive must be embraced with gratitude.

Towering over Williams and Miller is Eugene O'Neill (1888–1953), but his position in the mid-century American drama is a strange one. Although his final plays are now recognized as his masterpieces, they were either unknown or unappreciated then. Sick and embittered, O'Neill had withdrawn from the world, and his two plays produced during the 1940s, *The Iceman Cometh* (1946) and *A Moon for the Misbegotten* (1947), were unsuccessful. It would take another ten years, and his death, for him to be rediscovered, making the posthumous O'Neill more a playwright of the 1950s and 1960s. It was

A Streetcar Named Desire: Marlon Brando, Jessica Tandy. (Photo by Eileen Darby; courtesy of the Irene Mayer Selznick Collection, Twentieth Century Archives, Department of Special Collections, Boston University Library)

Williams and Miller who defined the serious American drama at midcentury; the pamphleteer of social issues and the poet of loneliness and fear were poles of a continuum on which most other dramatists of the late 1940s lay.

Among the already established writers, Lillian Hellman continued her practice of translating public issues into matters of private morality in *Another Part of the Forest* (1946) and an adaptation of Robles's *Montserrat* (1949). Sidney Kingsley's *Detective Story* (1949) presented a frightened man trying to cope with a world that wasn't as ordered as he thought, while Clifford Odets's *The Country Girl* (1950) dissected the psychology and power politics of an apparently doomed marriage. Few younger writers of the postwar period suggested major status. Arthur Laurents's *Home of the Brave* (1945) was a study of the psychological effects of anti-Semitism that put him alongside Miller in the socially conscious tradition of Odets and Kingsley, while William Inge's *Come Back, Little Sheba* (1950), like his later plays, presented little people who achieved some sort of happiness only by accepting their limitations; though considerably more sentimental than Williams, he shared his commitment to offering hope for emotional survival in a frightening world.

American comedy, always a staple of the Broadway theatre, shared the serious drama's focus on the present and familiar. The setting was generally contemporary America, more often than not the upper middle-class New York of the majority of the audience; the subject was generally romance; the comedy was generally that of situation and jokes, rather than physical farce or pure wit; and the plays were generally forgettable. The most successful Broadway comedy of the 1940s was actually a holdover from the previous decade: Howard Lindsay and Russel Crouse's adaptation of Clarence Day's *Life With Father*, the adventures of an unusual nineteenth-century family. Mary Ellen Chase's *Harvey* (1944), Garson Kanin's *Born Yesterday* (1946) and Norman Krasna's *John Loves Mary* (1947) were popular but ephemeral, though Joshua Logan and Thomas Heggen's *Mister Roberts* (1948) held enough sincere affection for its characters to give its string of wartime hijinks an emotional core.

There was also a third branch of the American drama. The Broadway musical ranks close behind jazz as one of America's

9

original contributions to world culture, and it was approaching its zenith at midcentury. Although historians can trace the form back to *The Black Crook*, an 1866 melodrama with interpolated songs and dances, the modern musical comedy is really a twentieth-century development. Its immediate ancestor was the lavish, waltz-filled Viennese costume operetta of the late nineteenth century, and many in the first generation of twentieth-century Broadway composers were European born (Rudolf Friml, Victor Herbert, Sigmund Romberg) or trained (Jerome Kern). The special American flavor came from the theatre's lively and vulgar cousin, vaudeville, particularly as filtered through the talent and sensibility of writer-composer-performer-producer George M. Cohan in the first decade of the century. As Cecil Smith explains,

> *Cohan's musical comedies introduced a wholly new conception of delivery, tempo, and subject matter into a form of entertainment that was rapidly dying for want of new ideas of any kind. Brushing aside the artificial elegances and the formal developments of the musical comedies based on English and German models, he reproduced successfully the hardness, the compensating sentimentality, the impulsive vulgarity, and the swift movement of New York life, which, except for surface sophistications, has not changed much between then and now.*[3]

The third significant ingredient was the instinct for spectacle of producer Florenz Ziegfeld, Jr., whose annual editions of the *Follies* between 1909 and 1927 developed an audience taste for big stars, pretty girls and lavish productions.

Between 1900 and 1920 these elements blended into something new—a light and spirited entertainment built on a flimsy, usually romantic plot and interrupted as often as possibly by songs ranging from ballads to elaborate production numbers. Smith quotes a cynical 1907 *Dramatic Mirror* review that could just as easily have been written twenty or even thirty years later:

> *Fascinating Flora is just another musical comedy built along the same lines as scores of its predecessors. Nothing but the expected happens: choruses sing, dance, stand in line, smile, wear colored clothes; principals get into trouble and out of it, burst into song at intervals commensurate with their impor-*

tance, make jokes about New York, do specialties of more or less cleverness; the curtain falls to divide the evening into two parts; the orchestra plays the air that the promoter hopes will be popular. The whole thing is done according to formula as accurately as a prescription is compounded in a drug store. And the audience . . . is pleased.[4]

The relative importance of story and songs in these shows is reflected in the convention, still prevalent, of crediting a musical to its songwriters even when the "book" is extraordinarily good; one thinks of Rodgers and Hammerstein's *South Pacific*, not Hammerstein and Logan's; Lerner and Loewe's *My Fair Lady*, not Shaw's. The importance of the music makes it extraordinarily fortunate that the most talented composers and lyricists were drawn to this form, and a list of Broadway musical collaborators from 1920 to 1950 is a pantheon of American popular music: Irving Berlin, Jerome Kern, George and Ira Gershwin, Cole Porter, Richard Rodgers, Lorenz Hart, Oscar Hammerstein, and so on.

The development of the musical was another positive product of the Broadway monopoly. It required a pool of talented performers and experienced producers, and the cross-fertilization of writers who could learn from and be challenged by each other. Moreover, as Smith suggested in his comment on George M. Cohan, in some only vaguely explainable way the musical seems to be the product of the New York City sensibility; virtually every major Broadway composer and lyricist since 1920 was born and raised in New York. (Even more curious and inexplicable is the fact that the overwhelming majority were Jewish.) With isolated exceptions, attempts at the musical form by artists from other parts of the country or other countries have lacked the special spark of the Broadway product.

Fortunately the Broadway product was exportable, and not only became a major representative of American theatre abroad, but also was the most accessible theatre to the majority of Americans. A hit musical might have two or three touring companies crossing the country during or after its Broadway run, making it the only experience of live professional theatre available in many places. Because of the talented composers and lyricists, and the glamor popularly associated with Broadway, theatre songs dominated American popular music until

11

the advent of rock and roll, with show tunes becoming national hits even though the majority of radio listeners or record buyers would never get a chance to see the play itself. As late as 1956, songs from *My Fair Lady* were recorded by dozens of popular singers, and more than twice as many people (over a million) bought the original cast recording in the first year than could possibly have seen the show.

The history of the musical from the 1920s to the 1950s is one of a gradual maturity in form and content, marked by an increasing inclination to break away from the formulas and conventions described in the 1907 *Fascinating Flora* review, and by attempts to deal with more serious subjects and complex characterizations. Kern and Hammerstein's *Show Boat* (1927), Rodgers and Hart's *Pal Joey* (1940), and Weill and Gershwin's *Lady in the Dark* (1941) were significant steps in this progress, but Rodgers and Hammerstein's *Oklahoma!* (1943) is generally considered the key landmark in the development of the genre. More than any of their predecessors Rodgers and Hammerstein succeeded in integrating the musical and nonmusical parts of the play, particularly through the use of "book songs" that took the place of spoken dialogue rather than just interrupting it, and through the introduction of dance sequences (choreographed by Agnes De Mille) that helped to develop plot or establish character rather than being self-justifying spectacle. The story of *Oklahoma!* was romantic but did include hints of dark psychological forces and the death of the villain at the hands of the hero; and the structure of the show broke with some of the stultifying conventions of earlier musicals, such as the obligatory opening production number and the chorus line of pretty girls.

Some of these innovations had appeared earlier, but this particular combination made the break with the past most dramatically. Writing in 1950, Oliver Smith wasn't even sure *Oklahoma!* was the same sort of animal as previous musicals:

> *The union of two sympathetic temperaments created the first all-American, non-Broadway musical comedy (or operetta; call it what you will) independent of the manners or traditions of Viennese comic opera or French opéra-bouffe on the one hand, and Forty-fourth Street clichés and specifications on the other.* Oklahoma! *turned out to be a people's opera.*[5]

And critics began to reach for new labels—the mature musical, the integrated musical, the musical play—to describe the new genre. The success of *Oklahoma!* led to many imitations in the next decade, some of them purely mechanical—for a period in the mid-1940s the insertion of a dream ballet in a musical comedy became as arbitrary and conventional a device as anything in *Fascinating Flora*—and some of them honorable attempts to explore and develop the possibilities of this new type of musical. Thus, just as Williams and Miller defined between them the serious American drama of 1950, Richard Rodgers and Oscar Hammerstein II dominated the American musical theatre.

Both men had begun writing in college, where they were acquainted, but their early careers were separate. Rodgers (1902–1979) teamed with lyricist Lorenz Hart, known for his worldly wit and inventive internal rhymes, and for twenty years wrote the music for such shows as *The Garrick Gaities, A Connecticut Yankee, The Boys from Syracuse* and *Pal Joey*. Meanwhile Hammerstein (1895–1960) leaned more toward the operetta edge of the musical theatre spectrum, writing lyrics for such composers as Jerome Kern (*Show Boat*), Rudolf Friml (*Rose Marie*) and Sigmund Romberg (*The Desert Song*). After their first collaboration on *Oklahoma!* the two produced *Carousel* (1945), the unsuccessful *Allegro* (1947) and *South Pacific* (1949); in the process they not only set very high standards for their competition to match, but also firmly established their style of musical—fully integrated in form, romantic but solidly dramatic in plot, entertaining but also inspirational in tone—as the norm.

In *South Pacific*, for example, most songs flow naturally and imperceptibly out of the dialogue—so much so that some critics thought the score undistinguished, failing to recognize the beauty and inevitable popularity of such songs as "Some Enchanted Evening" and "I'm Going to Wash That Man Right Out of My Hair" because they were so closely integrated with the plot and characters. The plot, based on short stories by James Michener, deals with two wartime love affairs threatened by racial prejudice, and thus has room for some serious social commentary. One story ends with the death of the man in combat while the other is resolved in reconciliation and hope, producing the honest sentiment and the inspiring tone that were Rodgers and Hammerstein's trademark.

Other successful musicals in the same spirit were Burton Lane and E. Y. Harburg's *Finian's Rainbow* (1947), in which an Irish leprechaun battled racial prejudice in the American

13

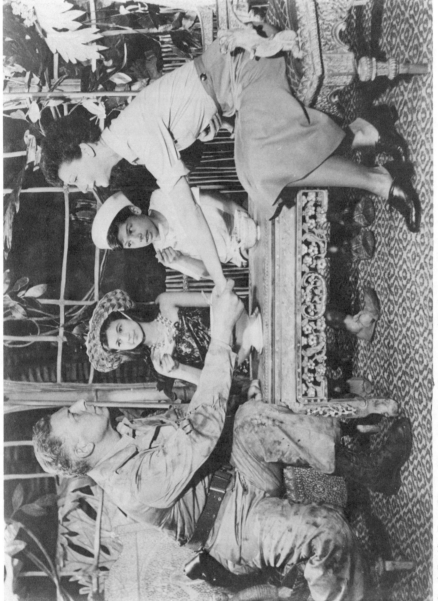

South Pacific: Ezio Pinza, Mary Martin. (Courtesy of Rodgers & Hammerstein)

South, and Alan Jay Lerner and Frederick Loewe's *Brigadoon* (1947), about an enchanted Scottish village that offered refuge to a man torn by the pressures of modern America. Cole Porter's characteristic mask of world-weary cynicism may have been more in tune with the 1930s than with the postwar years, but his *Kiss Me Kate* (1948) employed musical integration with a vengeance; the show followed the behind-the-scenes adventures of actors performing *The Taming of the Shrew*, and Porter's songs reflected the backstage and Shakespearean situations simultaneously. And if Irving Berlin's *Annie Get Your Gun* (1946) and Frank Loesser's *Guys and Dolls* (1950) were more elementary and old-fashioned in their construction, they just proved that the conventional musical comedy was still a vital genre, especially when a score included "There's No Business Like Show Business" or "Sit Down, You're Rocking the Boat."

As the American drama found its natural voice in realistic domestic melodrama, the American theatre found its natural style in a distinctively realistic mode of acting and production. The American style of acting, which has had a profound effect on world theatre and which symbiotically reinforced the native drama in its growth, is a special off-shoot of the revolution begun by the Russian director Konstantin Stanislavski at the end of the nineteenth century. Stanislavski's ideas were brought to America and transmuted into their American forms through several parallel channels. The Yiddish theatre movement in New York City, which flourished in the first twenty years of the century, was patterned after and strongly influenced by Stanislavski's Moscow Art Theatre, and it in turn influenced many American actors and directors. The Moscow Art Theatre itself first played in New York in 1923, and Stanislavski's *An Actor Prepares* was translated into English in 1936. The Group Theatre, one of the strongest "alternative" companies of the 1930s, was committed to Stanislavski; and when it disbanded in the mid-1940s, several of its members formed the Actor's Studio, which quickly became the most influential acting school in America. Other acting teachers of the late 1940s—notably Stella Adler (also a former Group member), Sanford Meisner and Aristide D'Angelo—were offering essentially the same approach to acting. But it is with the Actor's Studio and its director Lee Strasberg (1901–1982) that "The

15

Method," the American version of Stanislavski, is most closely associated.

The American Method is an extension of Stanislavski's suggestions to an actor preparing for a role. To oversimplify, Stanislavski taught that an actor faced with playing, say, a jealous man should recall occasions when he himself felt jealous and borrow attitudes, gestures and intonations from these experiences. The American Method, again to oversimplify, would have the actor hunt out the jealous side of his own personality, bring it to the fore so that in a controlled way he actually felt the emotion, and then behave naturally, as the emotion moved him. As David Garfield put it in a history of the Actor's Studio, Strasberg's "concept of acting [was] the creation of real experience in response to imaginary stimuli," and the results could transcend the limits of conscious acting, just as an effectively recreated memory of a lemon's taste can create actual salivation.[6] Method acting at its best could be devastatingly real and powerful, with actor and role blending into a totally believable performance. There was, inevitably, a price to be paid for this stress on psychological realism; as Garfield admits, "despite Strasberg's doctrinaire theorizing about the illimitable applicability of the Method approach, the truth is that the American Method simply does not have a record of accomplishment in the production of noncontemporary plays. Elia Kazan stated it quite directly in the early seventies when he said, 'We have not solved the classical acting problem. I failed with it.' "[7] In a modern realistic play an American-trained actor will almost certainly outshine a British actor of equal talent, but in Shakespeare, Restoration comedy or even Ibsen the British actor can rely on purely technical training that the American has not had. (Of course this has been noticed by acting schools on both sides of the Atlantic, who have adjusted their curricula accordingly, but the imbalance remains.)

The archetypal Method performance—and, to many who witnessed it, the greatest—was Marlon Brando's Stanley Kowalski in Williams's *Streetcar Named Desire*. Brando had previously appeared on Broadway in such varied roles as a homicidal soldier in *Truckline Cafe* (1946) and the sentimental poet Marchbanks in *Candida* (1946). But audiences were not prepared for the intense sexuality and the ability to communicate the passions and pains of an almost inarticulate character that

16

he brought to the Williams play. Except for a brief summer stock appearance in 1953 Brando never acted on a stage again, but the legendary stature of his Stanley, along with his film performances, fixed the new acting style—its faults and excesses as well as its virtues—in the public consciousness. Other Method-type actors of the period (not all of whom studied at the Actor's Studio) include Lee J. Cobb, Julie Harris, Geraldine Page, and Kim Stanley; and Garfield lists hundreds of Life Members of the Studio, crossing the generations from Franchot Tone to Al Pacino. Of course Broadway also had established stars of earlier generations: Katharine Cornell, Helen Hayes, Alfred Lunt and Lynn Fontaine, Frederick March and Florence Eldridge; and in musicals Ethel Merman, Mary Martin, Alfred Drake and Ray Bolger.

Realistic plays and realistic acting on proscenium stages imply realistic production styles, and a theatregoer attending a new play during this period could confidently expect the curtain to go up on a solid, real-looking set. For the most part Broadway sets, lighting and costumes were merely functional, though there were frequent attempts to reflect a play's emotional and psychological truth more than external verisimilitude for its own sake. Designer Jo Mielziner was particularly skilled at creating this sort of setting; the Loman house in *Death of a Salesman*, for example, was solid enough but placed and lit so that it faded into the shadows for the memory and fantasy sequences when the real location of the action was the inside of Willy's head.

Two directors earlier associated with the Group Theatre helped bring its methods (and The Method) to Broadway. Harold Clurman (b. 1901), who had directed many of the Group's most successful plays, was able to create a similar realism and ensemble playing in such Broadway productions as *The Member of the Wedding* (1950). Clurman also had a particularly acute visual sense, and created stage pictures and tableaux that embodied a play's meanings and remained in the audience's mind long afterward. Elia Kazan (b. 1909), director of both *Death of a Salesman* and *A Streetcar Named Desire*, was more dynamic. His method was to seek out the emotional core of a play and shape the staging and characterizations to its expression rather than to the surface plot; with *Streetcar*, for example, he decided that the backbone of the play was Blanche's experience of events, and structured each scene

17

Elia Kazan.
(Courtesy of Elia Kazan)

around her emotional state at that step in her decline. The result was a passionate intensity in the acting and a fluidity of action that carried audiences to the play's deeper emotional levels. Clurman's and Kazan's focus on a play's inner meanings and instinct for how they could be communicated on a stage helped the realistic American drama flourish in its maturity; and when Clurman left directing to become an influencial critic, Kazan became the most significant Broadway director of the 1950s. Two other successful directors were Joshua Logan, equally adept at drama, comedy and musicals, and frequently a collaborator in the writing of plays he directed; and George Abbott, who specialized in giving musicals and light comedies a rapid pace and inventive staging that enhanced good shows and disguised the weaknesses of poor ones.

Producing a Broadway play was an *ad hoc* operation. A producer got a likely script from an author or agent and contracted to put it on. He then raised the necessary money; hired a director, actors and staff (designers, press agent, etc.); rented a theatre; and oversaw the preparations. The director and actors rehearsed in rented halls while the set was built by a carpentry firm and the costumes were created or supplied by a costume company. When the show was ready it went on an out-of-town tour, on a circuit that usually included Philadelphia, Boston and New Haven, to be tested in front of audiences and revised if necessary. Then it opened in New York, was reviewed, and either closed in disgrace or ran for a while. The weekly operating surplus—the amount by which ticket sales exceeded running costs (rent, salaries, etc.)—was returned to the investors until they were repaid, and then was split between investors and producer. When a show stopped making a weekly profit it closed, and the entire organization was disbanded.

Unless a producer could put up his own money, producing meant finding "angels," investors who would supply the funds needed to meet the production's original expenses—royalties, preliminary salaries, set design and construction, theatre rental, etc. In 1950 these might amount to $60,000 for a straight play and over $200,000 for a musical. Angeldom was not an activity likely to attract a conservative banker; only one show in five made enough and ran long enough to recoup its initial investment before it closed, and the biggest hit might pay back three or four times its cost over a period of years—not bad, certainly, but given the odds, not the most prudent investment. So the Broadway investor was almost always someone with an emotional motive and not just a financial one—a commitment to the particular script or company, a love of theatre in general, or a desire to be part of the Broadway world. The successful producer probably had a list of such angels who had invested in previous shows of his with happy results. A new producer, or one who hadn't had many successes recently, might be forced to hunt out friends of friends, relatives of the author or names out of the social register. It was not uncommon for the composer and lyricist of a proposed new musical to perform the score at a series of parties in wealthy homes while the producer hovered in the background hoping that the guests would be moved to reach for their checkbooks.

Anyone could be a Broadway producer if he had a script and could raise the money, and in fact as many as 40 percent of each season's new shows were the work of new producers. In practice, though, most successful shows were produced by full-time professionals who maintained permanent offices and might have several projects at various stages of development simultaneously. The most active producing organization in the 1940s was the Theatre Guild, which offered several plays a year and raised much of its working capital by selling season

19

subscriptions in advance. Other prolific producers were John C. Wilson, Max Gordon and Michael Todd. While the producer's job was primarily a managerial one, he frequently took an active artistic role as well. It was the Theatre Guild, for example, that proposed that Rodgers and Hammerstein collaborate in adapting a play that the Guild had previously produced into a musical, and thus created *Oklahoma!* After their early successes Rodgers and Hammerstein formed their own producing organization to stage their musicals as well as other shows. The Playwrights' Company was a consortium of dramatists who produced their own plays; and directors (Kazan, Clurman, Abbott), performers (José Ferrer, Sonia Henie) and even theatre owners (the Shuberts) sometimes doubled as producers. However it was created, every Broadway show was an independent project involving dozens or even hundreds of unrelated artists and businessmen brought together solely for that occasion and disbanded when it closed.

In 1950 there were thousands of community theatre groups and college and university theatres across America, and it would be wrong to ignore them entirely. They satisfied the hunger for live theatre in communities far removed from Broadway and even from the routes of road companies. But there was no real continuity between the amateur and the professional theatre. Community theatre was not a breeding ground for new playwrights (though university theatre could be), nor were its part-time actors and directors likely to go on to professional work. Repertoires were made up almost entirely of recent Broadway hits, with an occasional classic, and even within that framework the amateur groups inevitably found light comedies and thrillers more attractive and more within their range than serious drama. Production and acting could be anything from nearly professional to awful, but the motivation was as much social (the fun of putting on a show or raising money for a worthy cause) or, in the colleges, educational as artistic, so the "success" of such ventures frequently had little to do with theatrical quality. Thus, while the community and academic theatres provided entertainment and a chance for self-expression for thousands of Americans, their real value was atheatrical, and they were a peripheral and generally sterile part of the American theatre.

There were some companies whose age, accomplishments

or ambitions made them outstanding. The Cleveland Play House, founded in 1916, and the Pasadena Community Playhouse, chartered in 1917, were amateur groups with professional directors and management. Both began as part of the art theatre movement of the period, devoted to producing classics and uncommercial plays, but through the years their repertoires became safer and more conventional. Still, the Cleveland Play House had premiered some plays that went on to Broadway runs; and the Pasadena group had one of the most ambitious schedules of any community theatre, and was also the home of a drama school, a branch of the University of California, that was the training ground of hundreds of New York and Hollywood actors. Two younger amateur companies—the Alley Theatre in Houston, founded in 1947, and the Arena Stage in Washington, D.C., founded in 1950—would become successful and respected enough to turn professional a few years later, signaling the rebirth of regional theatre.

There were some resident professional theatres outside New York, almost all summer stock companies providing unpretentious fare to undiscriminating vacationers; the Barter Theatre in Virginia, founded in 1932 and named the official State Theatre in 1941, represented this genre at its best. In Dallas, Theatre '50 was the first and only nonprofit resident repertory theatre in the country; it had opened (as Theatre '47) with the world premiere of Tennessee Williams's *Summer and Smoke*, but generally offered classics and revivals in two- or three-week runs.

Back in New York City, there was a theatrical alternative to Broadway, though the interested theatregoer might have to hunt to find it. There were about 150 non-Broadway productions in New York in the 1948–1949 season, but most were very short lived and virtually all were amateur, in fact or name, since Actors' Equity, the actors' union, set regulations and minimum salaries that the small companies could not meet. Equity occasionally looked the other way, especially for theatres that operated in the slow summer months, and in the summer of 1949 Equity negotiated an agreement with a group of Off-Broadway theatres that relaxed its requirements and encouraged professional Off-Broadway activity. Still, most of the almost 300 productions of the 1949–1950 season were limited to two or three performances, and many were little more

21

than auditions hoping to attract Broadway producers. Off-Broadway as a significant alternative was on the verge of appearing, but in 1950 it was still a fringe curiosity.

In the first week of January 1950 there were twenty-seven shows on Broadway: eight dramas, six comedies, eight musicals, three reviews, one ballet and an ice show. Among the plays were *Death of a Salesman*, *Detective Story*, *Mister Roberts*, *The Member of the Wedding*, Lunt and Fontaine in *I Know My Love*, and Katharine Cornell in *That Lady*. Musicals included *South Pacific*, *Kiss Me Kate*, *Where's Charley?* and *Gentlemen Prefer Blondes*. *A Streetcar Named Desire* and *Born Yesterday* had just closed; and *As You Like It* with Katharine Hepburn, *The Corn is Green* with Eva LeGallienne, and Eliot's *The Cocktail Party* were about to open. The dedicated theatregoer might know of some Off-Broadway theatres; the only one that could afford to advertise was a production of Strindberg's *Creditors*. And Sartre's *Respectful Prostitute*, which had begun Off-Broadway two seasons back and then had a Broadway run, was playing five times a day along with the movie in a Forty-second Street "grind house."

During the same week there were five productions in Philadelphia and five in Boston, either pre-Broadway tryouts or post-Broadway road companies, while Chicago had six road companies. *Mister Roberts* was playing in Kansas City, and *Oklahoma!* was in San Francisco. Tallulah Bankhead was touring Texas in *Private Lives*, playing two nights each in Houston, San Antonio and Fort Worth. Most of the rest of the country had no live theatre at all.

That was about to change.

Notes

1. Harold Clurman, Introd., *The Playwrights Speak*, ed. Walter Wager (New York: Dell Publishing Company, 1967), p. xiv.

2. Clurman, pp. xvii-xviii.

3. Cecil Smith, *Musical Comedy in America* (New York: Theatre Arts Books, 1950), p. 151.

4. Smith, p. 129.

5. Smith, pp. 343–44.

6. David Garfield, *A Player's Place* (New York: Macmillan, 1980), p. 175.

7. Garfield, pp. 181–82.

Off-Broadway

Off-Broadway was not an invention of the 1950s. There had been an alternative theatre of some sort in New York through most of the twentieth century. The same art theatre movement that gave birth to the amateur companies in Cleveland and Pasadena before World War I produced two notable New York companies that had brief professional lives. The Washington Square Players grew out of a play-reading group in the Liberal Club in 1914 and produced their first season of new American and European plays in 1915. They were successful enough to move to Broadway before the war brought a halt to their activities in 1918. The Provincetown Playhouse, an off-shoot of the Players, began as a summer theatre in Massachusetts and played intermittently in New York from 1916 to 1925. The 1920s saw Eva LeGallienne's Civic Repertory Theatre, and the 1930s produced left-leaning socially conscious companies such as the Worker's Drama League and the Theatre Collective, as well as the several units of the government-sponsored Federal Theatre.

Two theatrical traditions that are not normally thought of as part of Off-Broadway are worth mentioning here. The Yiddish Theatre was a vital force in the lives of New York's immigrant Jewish population for almost fifty years. Such actor-managers as Maurice Schwartz, Jacob Ben-Ami and Boris Thomashevsky led repertory companies that offered quality productions of

Shakespeare, Gogol, Strindberg and other European masters as well as the plays of Jewish writers. And the short-lived "Harlem Renaissance" that peaked in the 1920s was reflected in a flourishing theatre district in New York's black community, where the Alhambra, Lafayette, Lincoln and Crescent Theatres produced plays, many since lost, written by black authors for black audiences.

But none of these companies was able to create a lasting and fruitful alternative to the Broadway monopoly. Some, like the black theatres of the 1920s and the workers' theatres of the 1930s, were products of their time and died when their era was over. The others all fed into Broadway instead of growing apart from it. The Washington Square Players and the Provincetown Playhouse are historical footnotes whose greatest importance lies in the fact that the first evolved after 1920 into the Theatre Guild, one of the most active Broadway producing organizations of the next forty years, while the second produced the early plays of Eugene O'Neill. The Yiddish Theatre died out as its audience became Americanized, but it had served as a bridge between the European theatre—particularly the Moscow Art Theatre, on which several Yiddish companies were modeled—and the American. It also played an important role in nurturing the love of theatre in New York City's Jewish population, which has subsequently made up a disproportionately large segment of the Broadway audience.

The most influential alternative company of the 1930s was the Group Theatre, which actually operated on Broadway. It spoke more effectively than any other theatre for the disaffected, left-leaning generation of the Depression, and introduced the plays of Clifford Odets and Sidney Kingsley. But even its real importance lies in its contribution to Broadway, in the professionalism, social awareness and commitment to Stanislavski that its members brought to their later work. Director and critic Harold Clurman, director Elia Kazan, producer Cheryl Crawford, and teachers Lee Strasberg and Stella Adler, all Group alumni, played important roles in shaping the mainstream (i.e., Broadway) theatre of the postwar years.

The Off-Broadway movement of the 1950s was different in that its influence rippled outward. Although its own most vital period lasted only about fifteen years, it directly and indirectly spawned other alternative movements throughout the country. Off-Broadway broke the Broadway monopoly in the public perception and created room for other possibilities. The generation of young actors who got their start Off-Broadway in the 1950s produced the major film and theatre stars of the next decade; and younger actors, seeing that Broadway was not the only place to make a career, found growth and challenges in regional theatres. Audiences around the country heard the recording of the Off-Broadway *Threepenny Opera* or saw touring companies of *The Fantasticks*, discovered that they were as entertaining and approachable as any Broadway musical, and were more receptive to the next play carrying the Off-Broadway label. Producers and civic leaders around the country sensed this increased theatrical interest and fed it by establishing theatres and companies to match the excitement of Off-Broadway. And even as Off-Broadway's innovative fervor began to wane in the 1960s another generation of ambitious and experimental theatre artists followed its lead and created Off Off-Broadway as an alternative to the alternative. All this activity encouraged young writers, particularly those interested in exploring styles and ideas that did not fit into the Broadway mainstream, and the best dramatic writing of the 1960s and 1970s was first staged someplace other than Broadway. Off-Broadway itself produced plays, styles and individual artists of importance, but its greatest significance lies in the alternative it created and the other alternatives it inspired.

The history of this Off-Broadway movement can be divided into three periods. The first, from about 1950 to 1958, saw the birth of the alternative theatre in the formation of several key companies whose successes attracted audiences and began the careers of a generation of actors. Noticeably missing in this period are new American playwrights, since the repertoire was dominated by classics, revivals and American premieres of modern European plays. The second period, roughly 1959 to 1966, redressed this imbalance as a generation of young American dramatists were discovered and their plays produced. Although this renaissance proved somewhat abortive, with many of the writers unable to live up to the promise of their first works, the period of excitement led New York and regional theatres to seek out and encourage other young writers of their own, expanding the ripple effect of Off-Broadway. Finally, from the late 1960s on, Off-Broadway's revolutionary significance waned and it evolved into a valid alternative in the expanded mainstream, the home of plays and

25

productions which might not be inherently different in form and content from those on Broadway or in regional theatres, but which were more appropriate to smaller theatres, more modest budgets and more sophisticated audiences.

Most of the hundreds of non-Broadway productions in New York in the years immediately following World War II were not really part of Off-Broadway. Many were amateur or student efforts, and some were vanity exercises subsidized by the stage-struck participants or their loving families. A large number were one- or two-performance showcases for authors or actors hoping to attract the attention of Broadway producers. The growth of a professional alternative theatre was hampered by the fact that Actors' Equity forbade its members to work alongside nonmembers and demanded minimum salaries which, however modest, were beyond the shoestring budgets of most non-Broadway companies.

Still, actors want to act, and acting for five dollars a week or even for nothing seemed better to many young performers than not acting at all. Increasingly toward the end of the 1940s Equity was forced to look the other way as its members violated its regulations to appear in Off-Broadway productions. In 1949 five professional companies—Interplayers, Off-Broadway Incorporated, People's Drama, Studio Seven and We Present—united to form the Off-Broadway Theatre League and negotiated an agreement with Equity that allowed union actors to appear with nonmembers as long as a token salary was paid. The Off-Broadway movement of the 1950s was born.

Nothing happened overnight, of course. There was no proven audience for Off-Broadway, and thus little to attract experienced Broadway producers and investors. (The first major Broadway producer to venture Off-Broadway, Kermit Bloomgarden, waited until 1961 to do so.) The young actors and directors who wanted to work Off-Broadway had to become producers as well; and it was typical of this Off-Broadway generation that its members did not come together to put on single plays, but to form what were meant to be continuing companies, complete in many cases with artistic manifestos declaring their commitment "to release actors, directors, playwrights and designers from the pressures forced on them by the hit-or-flop pattern of Broadway [and] to provide for the public a playhouse within the means of everyone"[1] (Phoenix

Theatre); or "to create a style of acting not too internal, not too bombastic, so that poetic plays could be done on the stage in a highly realistic way, without sacrificing the poetry and the style"[2] (New York Shakespeare Festival); or "to explore untried methods and techniques for the extension of the boundaries of theatrical expression"[3] (Living Theatre).

Economics and tradition lured most of these young artists to Greenwich Village, the bohemian district in the southern part of Manhattan, roughly where old New Amsterdam ends and the numbered streets begin. Some operated in existing theatres such as the Cherry Lane and the Provincetown Playhouse, while others created playing spaces in vacant lofts, nightclubs and movie houses. Budgets ranged from zero to a few thousand dollars for an entire season, at a time when a single Broadway play cost $60,000 or more. They supported themselves with nontheatrical jobs, scrounged materials and props from friends and trash piles, and maneuvered their way through or around fire and zoning regulations. Many of their histories resemble the plots of the Mickey Rooney–Judy Garland movies of the 1940s, and there is no doubt that youthful innocence and exuberance led them to successes that wiser heads would have considered impossible.

Four especially significant companies were born at this time: the Circle in the Square, the Living Theatre, the Phoenix Theatre and the New York Shakespeare Festival. Only part of their importance lies in the work they produced in their early years; much of it is in the patterns they set for other groups in New York and elsewhere. Each of the four had a different beginning, style and philosophy; and each evolved through several stages in the next twenty years. Their similarities and differences mark the general outlines of the Off-Broadway movement in its first period, outlines that they helped form through their influence on others.

The roots of the Circle in the Square are very much in the "Hey , kids, let's put on a show!" traditon. In the late 1940s a group of young actors took over an old theatre in Woodstock, New York, for several summer seasons. By 1950 their number included Panamanian-born director José Quintero (b. 1924) and business manager Theodore Mann (b. 1924), who were among the core group determined to form a permanent theatre in New York City. They rented a former nightclub in Greenwich Village's Sheridan Square, converted its circular

The Circle in the Square:
José Quintero.
(Photo by Martha Swope)

dance floor into a three-sided arena stage, and named it the Circle in the Square. They lived commune-style in rooms above the theatre and put on a series of modern European and American plays, passing the hat after performances until they overcame licensing restrictions that kept them from selling tickets as a real theatre. In April 1952 they revived Tennessee Williams's *Summer and Smoke,* which had failed on Broadway in 1948, and found themselves with Off-Broadway's first smash hit.

Much of the credit for the Circle's early success must go to its director. José Quintero was not a methodical analyst and theoretician as Clurman and Kazan were, or a master of pure technique, as Abbott was. He operated through instinct and through a total emotional commitment to his work that freed his imagination and sensitivity. In his memoirs he recalled his first visit to the garishly painted nightclub that would become his theatre:

> *Looking at one of the walls, I saw a painted leopard. I permitted him to become real for a few seconds. . . . He began to circle the center pole where I was standing, then proceeded in a series of*

*curves until he reached the farthest poles of the arena. . . . The
leopard never walked a straight line. He curved himself around as
he walked, almost in the shape of an S. At that moment I began to
understand the kind of movement that the three-quarter arena
demanded.*[4]

The Circle in the Square was not the first nonproscenium
theatre in America, but Quintero was the first to sense that
arena staging was not just a matter of audience placement but
required a wholly new kind of blocking and movement, that
the straight crossings and diagonals of the proscenium stage
must be replaced by wide arcs and more circular motions, to
reflect the audience's sense of the room they were in. Quintero
also saw that the company's poverty freed it from the solid sets
and realistic props of the commercial theatre, and that an
almost bare stage would challenge and liberate the imaginations of actors and audience. Certainly one of the direct lega-
cies of Off-Broadway was the discovery that theatre could
happen in unconventional spaces, and Quintero's discoveries
of how such spaces could reshape acting and production styles
were seminal.

Quintero demanded the same sort of complete freedom of
the imagination from his actors, using a childhood memory of
a circus clown kissing a member of the audience as a model of
the kind of emotional openness he wanted. Directing was a
matter of guiding the performers toward the confidence and
identification with their roles that would allow them to take
such emotional risks. Quintero's account of the rehearsals for
Eugene O'Neill's *Long Day's Journey into Night* is filled with
extended discussions and arguments with and between the
actors *in character*, and with almost confessional statements
and anecdotes by the director designed both to communicate a
particular mood and to encourage the actors toward similar
self-exposure.[5] There was little attention to mechanics in Quintero rehearsals; if the actors found the truth of their roles and
the ability to express it honestly, he was sure line readings and
movements would follow naturally.

Quintero was thus more dependent on his actors than a
more doctrinaire director would be, and he was fortunate in
having a pool of young, determined and talented performers
to work with. The star of *Summer and Smoke* was Geraldine
Page in her first big New York role after several years in

29

Eugene O'Neill. (Courtesy of the Billy Rose Theatre Collection, The New York Public Library at Lincoln Center. Astor, Lenox and Tilden Foundations)

summer stock. Jason Robards, Jr. got the starring role in the Circle's second great success, O'Neill's *The Iceman Cometh*, by demanding it and by auditioning with a dynamic reading that convinced Quintero that the tall, thin young actor could make the audience see O'Neill's fat and aging protagonist. Peter Falk played a small role in *Iceman*; and Colleen Dewhurst, Salome Jens, George C. Scott and George Segal were also among the Circle's alumni in its first decade.

The Circle's *Iceman Cometh*, which ran from 1956 to 1958, was important for another reason: it was the direct and immediate cause of America's rediscovery of its greatest dramatic genius. Eugene O'Neill's reputation was made in the 1920s with such experimental and nonnaturalistic plays as *The Hairy Ape* and *Strange Interlude*, which seemed dated and unplayable thirty years later. Although O'Neill had returned to realism in his later plays, he had not released most of them for production, and his two plays produced in the 1940s, *The Iceman Cometh* and *A Moon for the Misbegotten*, had been failures. The Circle's *Iceman*, thanks to Quintero's direction and Robards's bravura performance, proved that O'Neill was not a dated experimenter but a great naturalistic writer with a vision that was evidently particularly meaningful to the Cold War generation. The message of *Iceman*—that self-delusion, however crippling or degrading it may be, is nonetheless absolutely essential to survival, since man is simply unequipped to deal with the naked horrors of reality—had seemed nihilistic in 1946, but was welcomed as a key to self-acceptance and self-forgiveness ten years later, as audiences responded to O'Neill's argument that we must not feel guilty about a need as basic and inescapable as those for food and shelter.

O'Neill's widow and literary executor had taken a liking to Quintero and was so impressed by his production of *Iceman* that she offered him an unproduced O'Neill play, *Long Day's Journey into Night*, which Quintero directed on Broadway in 1956. O'Neill had intended to keep *Long Day's Journey* secret until twenty-five years after his death, so it is directly to Quintero and the Circle that we owe the availability of what is almost certainly the greatest of all American plays. Even more purely than *Iceman*, *Long Day's Journey* is a play of forgiveness and reassurance, facing man's inherent limitations and finding comfort in the realization that his failure to be perfect is not his fault. That the play is undisguisedly autobiographical, using O'Neill's own tormented family as its metaphor, only makes the courage of his search for truth and the charity of his sharing his discovery that much more overwhelming. *Long Day's Journey into Night* was followed in turn by other posthumous plays and revivals, confirming the discovery that O'Neill's return to realism in his later career produced his and the American drama's true masterpieces.

The Circle in the Square was born out of the desire of young and talented people to work. Its choice of plays was determined by available performers and personal enthusiasms rather than by a particular social or artistic position. Although the talent of its director and of the actors who appeared regularly helped it develop an identity and style, that result was unpremeditated. In their own ways the other three seminal Off-Broadway companies were generated by specific literary, theatrical or philosophical ideals. As a result each was somewhat more a direct reflection of its founders' personalities, strengths and obsessions.

The roots of the Living Theatre go back to 1946 when artist Julian Beck (b. 1925) and his wife, actress Judith Malina (b. 1926), began to theorize about a new kind of theatre. Their early statements and manifestos show that they were not really sure what form this new production style would take,

31

Long Day's Journey into Night: Florence Eldridge, Bradford Dillman, Jason Robards Jr., Frederick March. (Courtesy of The Homer Dickens Collection)

except that it should break with the conventions of the commercial theatre and somehow reflect the vitality and evocative
power of modern art. As late as 1959 Julian Beck expressed
himself in terms more theoretical than practical, showing that
they hadn't gone far beyond being sure what they *didn't* want
to do, and incidently proving that the very mystical turn their
later work took was not an accident:

> With obstinate devotion we believe in the theatre as a place of
> intense experience, half-dream half-ritual, in which the spectator
> approaches something of a vision of self-understanding, going
> past the conscious to the unconscious, to an understanding of the
> nature of all things. . . . That is why at The Living Theatre we
> are trying to work beyond the limitations of realistic techniques of
> staging and of acting.[6]

In their search for material of high literary quality that would
also help them explore the boundaries of the theatrical experience, the Becks were drawn at first to poetic and nonlinear
drama. Their first production, in 1948, was an Ezra Pound
adaptation of Noh drama, and they officially opened the Living Theatre in 1951 with Gertrude Stein's *Doctor Faustus Lights
the Lights*. For the next decade their repertoire was dominated
by such writers as Stein, Eliot, Picasso and Cocteau.

Chronically impoverished, the Becks operated out of cellars,
lofts and theatres all over Manhattan, even giving one brief
season in their own living room; and they were subject to long
silent periods when they had no money and no theatre. All the
Living Theatre's productions from 1951 to 1960 totaled only
1000 performances, and more than half of those were in the
1959–1960 season. Obviously the Living Theatre was much
slower in achieving popular success than the Circle in the
Square, and its real contributions began in the second period
of Off-Broadway's history. But even during the 1950s the close
identification of the Living Theatre's work with the passions
and personalities of the Becks, along with its conscious dedication to the expansion of the theatrical repertoire and vocabulary, helped shape the identity and power of Off-Broadway.
The image of Off-Broadway as a place where bohemian mys-
tics performed strange plays in curious settings was an almost
immediate caricature in the public perception, but like all
caricatures it reflected a part of reality. And the reality or the

The Living Theatre 1961. Front: playwright Jack Gelber, directors Julian Beck and Judith Malina. Rear: choreographer Merce Cunningham, stage manager Peter Feldman, administrator James Spicer. (Courtesy of the Billy Rose Theatre Collection, The New York Public Library at Lincoln Center. Astor, Lenox and Tilden Foundations)

caricature was an inspiration and model to other young dreamers who began to realize that they too might be able to explore their theatrical ideas outside the Broadway mainstream. Once the Living Theatre achieved success and then notoriety, its influence would be even greater and more direct.

If the Becks were visionaries, the founders of the Phoenix Theatre were solid professionals. Norris Houghton (b. 1909) and T. Edward Hambleton (b. 1911) each had had twenty years' experience in various aspects of commercial theatre when they combined forces to form an alternative art theatre that could produce uncommercial plays. They took over a 1200 seat theatre on the edge of Greenwich Village, drew on their Broadway contacts for their initial financial support, and opened the Phoenix Theatre in 1953. The Phoenix repertoire leaned heavily on classics and revivals, with the added attraction of established stars such as Montgomery Clift, Hume Cronyn, Robert Ryan, Jessica Tandy and Nancy Walker. Given such casts and the commercial experience of the two producers, they were perhaps a bit disingenuous when they said, "The Phoenix was by no means founded as a proving ground for possible Broadway hits. But if one of our productions is judged worthy of moving to Broadway, . . . we see nothing wrong with that."[7]

Despite individual critical successes, the Phoenix's early seasons lost thousands of dollars, and any plan of supporting the theatre by Broadway transfers never worked out. Still, the absolute dedication of Houghton and Hambleton kept it alive even if, true to its name, it had to be reborn in a new form every few years. First they merged with a moribund theatre club to gain its subscription list and nonprofit status. For two seasons (1959–1961) they established and maintained a resident repertory company. In 1961 the Phoenix moved to a smaller and more economical theatre. In 1964 it combined forces with the Association of Producing Artists, a Michigan-based touring repertory company, and offered Broadway seasons, the Phoenix providing the organization and the APA the plays. While this partnership led to some striking productions and the brief return of rotating repertory to Broadway, its awkwardness (Who was in charge of what?) and the differing personal and corporate styles of Phoenix director Hambleton and APA director Ellis Rabb led to increasing difficulties and deficits, and the partnership was dissolved in 1969. The APA soon broke

35

The Phoenix Theatre: T. Edward Hambleton and Norris Houghton, with director-choreographer Jerome Robbins. (Courtesy of the Phoenix Theatre)

up, while the Phoenix returned to producing, first on Broadway, then as a touring company with a repertory of classics, then as an Off-Broadway theatre devoted to new plays, dying and rising in a new manifestation at regular intervals. As Stuart W. Little noted,

Throughout its history the Phoenix . . . occupied an anomalous position somewhere between Broadway and off-Broadway in size, somewhere between New York and regional theatre in sophistication, somewhere between the commercial and the art theater in audience appeal, . . . somewhere between the contemporary theater and the classic in the thrust of its programming. . . . By adaptation and structural change the Phoenix repeatedly found the means of survival.[8]

And in every manifestation the Phoenix maintained high standards of professionalism that counterbalanced the inexperience of many Off-Broadway companies. If the Phoenix never had the major hits or the colorfulness of some other theatres, its continuity and relative orthodoxy helped give Off-Broadway legitimacy in the eyes of more conservative audiences.

The guiding spirit of the New York Shakespeare Festival is Joseph Papp (b. 1921), a unique figure combining in his own way the theatrical instincts of Quintero, the vision of the Becks and the practical expertise of Houghton and Hambleton. Papp may be the American theatre's nearest approach to a Diaghilev, a workoholic totally dedicated to his theatre and as skilled in raising money and manipulating civic authorities as he is in spotting and supporting artistic talent in others. As a young and undistinguished theatre and television director in the early 1950s he had the vision of a new American style of Shakespearean production that would give classical acting the naturalness and vitality that the Method had given contemporary drama. At the same time he felt an almost messianic commitment to making Shakespeare freely available to what he called "a great dispossessed audience—both the ordinary theatregoers who have been priced out of the theatre, and those who have never seen a live professional production."[9] He founded his Shakespeare Workshop in a Lower East-Side church in 1954, and in the summer of 1956 gave his first season of free Shakespeare in the bandshell of a nearby park, on a trailer truck that traveled throughout the city, and finally in

The New York Shakespeare Festival: Joseph Papp. (Courtesy of The New York Shakespeare Festival)

Central Park. After a legal skirmish in 1959 with the parks commissioner, who feared that the free performances would bring an undesirable element into his parks to trample on his grass, Papp convinced the city and philanthropist George Delacorte to build him a permanent outdoor Central Park theatre, where the New York Shakespeare Festival has provided free summer seasons ever since.

In the years that followed, Papp's limitless energy and vision would lead the New York Shakespeare Festival to a permanent year-round home, seasons of award-winning new plays and classics, traveling theatre-in-the-streets companies, television productions, and artistic and commercial successes on, Off- and Off Off-Broadway. In the 1950s his contribution was in creating another noncommercial alternative to Broadway and in providing a place for the Off-Broadway generation of actors and directors to find their way into Shakespeare; among his early actors were Roscoe Lee Browne, Colleen Dewhurst, James Earl Jones and George C. Scott. And as that list suggests, Papp also pioneered a colorblind philosophy of casting that expanded the range of roles available to black and Hispanic actors while also liberating the imaginations of audiences, who quickly adjusted to the sight of a black Lear with white daughters or a mixed-race Roman senate.

There were other notable Off-Broadway companies during this first decade, many of which had commercial and artistic successes that helped increase public awareness of the alternative theatre. The Shakespearewrights, founded and supported by Shakespeare lover Donald Goldman in 1953, anticipated and paralleled Joseph Papp's work with productions designed to be clean, clear and entertaining, frequently performed for high school and college audiences. David Ross led the 4th Street Theatre through a successful cycle of Chekhov plays, while the Irish Players explored that national dramatic heritage. There were individual hits as well. The biggest, and up to that time the longest-running musical in New York theatre history, was Marc Blitzstein's adaptation of Kurt Weill and Bertolt Brecht's *The Threepenny Opera*. The satiric musical opened for a brief run in March 1954 as part of a repertory season at the Theatre de Lys, and then reopened in September 1955 and ran for over six years. Blitzstein's version softened some of the anger in Brecht's depiction of criminal society as a logical extension of the capitalist system, which may have helped make the play acceptable to American audiences. Weill's alternately brassy and haunting music, the intimacy of the tiny theatre, and a strong cast led by Weill's widow Lotte Lenya in the role she had created in 1928 also contributed to making this still the most successful American production of any of Brecht's plays. The original cast album sold hundreds of thousands of copies, and "The Ballad of Mack the Knife" was a popular hit for almost every singer who recorded it.

The Threepenny Opera was also an early hint of the direction toward which Off-Broadway would evolve. Although its small theatre and modest production were keys to a success it probably would not have had on Broadway, it was not inherently different from the Broadway product but rather a variant of it. While it was still running, critic Robert Brustein complained in a different context that "Off Broadway was originally established as an alternative theatre for serious works of art. . . . The accumulation of musicals in the minority theatre is a depressing sign of commercial accommodation."[10] Increasingly in the following years Off-Broadway would take a shape that was not so much an alternative to Broadway as an alternative version of it.

39

In addition to the actors and actresses already mentioned, the generation that got its start or early experience Off-Broadway during this period included Beatrice Arthur, Ben Gazzara, Joel Grey, Tammy Grimes, Hal Holbrook, Jack Palance and Kim Stanley. (Off-Broadway continued to be a breeding ground of future stars: the 1960s produced, among others, Faye Dunaway, Dustin Hoffman, Stacy Keach, Frank Langella and Al Pacino; the 1970s Judd Hirsch, William Hurt, Michael Moriarty, Christopher Reeve, Meryl Streep and Sigourney Weaver.) Other than José Quintero, the most successful Off-Broadway director of the 1950s was Stuart Vaughan (b. 1925), who began with the New York Shakespeare Festival and directed the Phoenix Theatre during its two-year experiment as a repertory company. The cornerstone of Joseph Papp's attempt to create an American style of producing Shakespeare, Vaughan filled the plays with movement and inventive business, although he was only intermittently successful in helping untrained actors handle the verse. His most successful work at the Phoenix was also in Shakespeare, and his experience in organizing and operating one of the first large-scale repertory companies in contemporary America led to a career in the regional theatre movement.

The London production of John Osborne's *Look Back in Anger* in 1956 introduced a revolutionary new voice into the staid and conventional British theatre, and the next few years showed that there was a whole generation of young dramatists with new things to say and new dramatic vocabularies to express them in. There was no equivalently shocking moment in the American theatre, but the same years produced a comparable group of new young American dramatists whose plays gave shape to the second stage in Off-Broadway's development. The generating factor in America may have been the discovery of the important new European playwrights, itself one of Off-Broadway's significant contributions. Samuel Beckett's *Waiting for Godot* was produced on Broadway in 1956, but his other plays received their first American productions Off-Broadway, starting with *Endgame* in 1959, *Krapp's Last Tape* in 1960 and *Happy Days* in 1961. Eugene Ionesco's *The Lesson* and *The Chairs* were produced by the Phoenix Theatre in 1958, and *The Bald Soprano* appeared Off-Broadway in the same year. In addition to *The Threepenny Opera*, Brecht was represented by the Phoenix's *Good Woman of Setzuan* in 1956 and the Living Theatre's *In the Jungle of Cities* in 1961; and Jean Genêt's *The Balcony* was a big success for the Circle in the Square in 1960.

The first indication that a new generation of American writers was going to challenge the conventions of Broadway drama came in 1959, when the Living Theatre produced Jack Gelber's *The Connection*. Gelber (b. 1931) showed a group of heroin addicts waiting for their dealer to arrive, in what was not only a shocking piece of social realism but also a series of challenges to middle-class complacency. Although his junkies were clearly burned out and unsalvageable, they could be eloquent and even persuasive in their praise of the fix and in their argument that heroin addiction is just a variant on more accepted compulsions toward sex, money or power. The form of the play also threatened comfortable preconceptions: Gelber's premise was that a playwright had cast real junkies in his play about junkies, and their refusal to follow the script attacked the audience's expectation of the sort of safe, controlled, comfortable theatrical experience that conventional theatres offered.

The Connection was a major turning point for the Living Theatre. By accident more than design their 1959 season was made up of three plays set in the theatre: Pirandello's *Tonight We Improvise*, William Carlos Williams's *Many Loves* and *The Connection*. This coincidence helped Beck and Malina find the "extension of the boundaries of theatrical expression" that they had declared as a goal and had been feeling their way toward for a decade. From this point on the Living Theatre would be committed to breaking down the comfortable distance between audience and play, and would directly influence the styles of companies and directors throughout the world.

The staging of *The Connection* was designed to reinforce the script's threats to complacency. The audience entering the theatre found the performers already there, involved in improvised actions and conversations that imperceptibly moved into the start of the play. Musicians in the group broke into improvised jazz pieces at seemingly random moments. During intermission the actors stayed in character and mingled with the audience, engaging in conversations, starting arguments and demanding handouts. The interruptions of the "playwright" when the junkies refused to follow his script seemed unre-

41

hearsed, while the onstage depictions of the mechanics of shooting up and the results of an overdose were frighteningly real. Even the most sophisticated theatregoers had to leave the play uncertain whether those actually were real addicts and whether everything that happened had been part of the script.

The Connection was not an immediate success and was kept alive in the repertoire by the more popular *Many Loves* for the first few weeks of its run. But as word of this new play and this challenging theatrical experience spread, everyone who was interested in theatre wanted to see it. *The Connection* became the mainstay of the Living Theatre's next few seasons and of its European tours in 1961 and 1962. More than that, it signaled a new identity for Off-Broadway as a home for the avant-garde in plays and productions, and its style and staging devices were widely imitated. But the Living Theatre could not enjoy this success for long. In 1963 the company staged Kenneth Brown's *The Brig*, a critical picture of life in a Marine stockade, in a brutal and unrelenting production designed to exhaust and frighten the audience rather than entertain them. In the intervening years the Becks had become active in the fledgling antiwar movement, and when the Internal Revenue Service seized their theatre in October 1963 for failure to pay back taxes, they were convinced that they were being punished for their unpatriotic play and behavior, and resisted. Their arrest and trial only reinforced their belief that the government was repressing their art for political reasons, and after their conviction and brief imprisonment—actually, the sympathetic judge allowed them to play a London engagement before returning to serve their terms—the Becks exiled themselves and their company to Europe, where the Living Theatre evolved again into a new form that would once more shake theatrical preconceptions when it returned to America in 1968.

Meanwhile, other new voices were being heard. *The Zoo Story* by Edward Albee (b. 1928), first produced in Berlin in 1959, had its American premiere Off-Broadway in January 1960. *The Sandbox* opened in May, *The American Dream* the following January, and *The Death of Bessie Smith* in March 1961. Albee's Off-Broadway plays were clearly the work of a beginning writer, but one whose talent and distinctive voice overcame his technical limitations. He owed obvious debts to older writers, most notably to Ionesco in *The American Dream* and to Tennessee Williams in his sympathy for social outcasts and his poetic and musical use of language; and he repeatedly fell into the trap of long, essentially nondramatic monologues. But the plays also showed a striking control of language and a startling new view of contemporary America as a threatening and spirit-destroying place.

The Zoo Story and *The American Dream* are the strongest of the four. In the first a comfortable, middle-class executive sitting on a park bench is accosted by a troubled young man who launches into an extended monologue describing his rootless, haunted life and his desperate need to make contact with someone or something that will convince him of his own reality. He finds that comfort only in death when his story destroys the executive's complacency and leads to a mortal battle over possession of the bench. In *The American Dream* the conversation of an archetypal American family—Mommy, Daddy, Grandma and a Young Man—echoes the banalities and absurdities of Ionesco's *Bald Soprano,* particularly in the literal use of metaphors and clichés. But Albee presents this linguistic abuse as a symptom of their misuse of each other: both language and social norms are consciously used to deny the value of the individual, and the American Dream is of sterile and lifeless beauty.

Albee's four short Off-Broadway plays showed him to be a writer of considerable promise. His first full-length play, produced on Broadway in 1962, established him as the most important American dramatist since Miller and Williams. *Who's Afraid of Virginia Woolf?* is one of the very best plays in the American repertoire, and was the first to fit the new Off-Broadway sensibility into the conventions of mainstream Broadway drama. A realistic domestic melodrama with four characters, a single set and a fictional time identical to its playing time, it is both frightening and inspirational in its depiction of contemporary America. Albee's protagonists George and Martha are a middle-aged couple apparently trapped in a Strindbergian marriage built on lies, fantasies, infidelities and alcohol. They spend much of the play attacking each other with brilliantly caustic wit, and horrify the younger couple who are their houseguests for a night of abusive and damaging psychological games. But through all the horrors Albee makes us see that this marriage *works*—that it supports, reinforces and protects, keeping George and Martha alive and able to cope with the pains and frustrations of life. Meanwhile,

Who's Afraid of Virginia Woolf? Margo Skinner, Richard Kneeland (Trinity Square Repertory Company). (Courtesy of Trinity Square Repertory Company)

the supposedly healthier marriage of their guests is exposed as
false and cowardly, devoted to escape from the challenges of
reality rather than support for dealing with them. George and
Martha experience life as the young man in *The Zoo Story* does,
but they have found the life-supporting connection he was
searching for; and Albee warns that we must not allow this
marriage's imperfections (to put it mildly) to blind us to how
necessary it is to its partners' spiritual and psychological survival.

None of Albee's later plays had the power or success of
Virginia Woolf, though *Tiny Alice* (1964) was an intriguing if
somewhat obscure exploration into the demands of religious
faith, and *A Delicate Balance* (1966) was an effective restatement
of his conviction that relationships that provide some support
in coping with a frightening universe must be preserved whatever their imperfections. Still, as Little notes,

> *Edward Albee more than anyone else opened up off-Broadway to*
> *new writers. It was partly his visible success that gave encour-*
> *agement to new writers. . . . It was also the quality and the*
> *character of his writing that alerted the theater and excited and*
> *challenged his contemporaries. For he had opened a new vein of*
> *dramatic writing.*[11]

In fact, Albee's success had an even more direct benefit for
Off-Broadway writers. His producers, Richard Barr and Clinton Wilder, were committed to the presentation of new plays,
and Albee joined with them in devoting some of *Virginia
Woolf*'s profits to the establishment of a Playwrights Unit, a
workshop for young dramatists where their work could be
read, analysed and given modest stagings. Practically every
notable young American dramatist of the 1960s passed
through the Playwrights Unit, and several had their work
commercially produced by its sponsors. Two star graduates
were LeRoi Jones and Mart Crowley. In Jones's best play,
Dutchman (1964), a white seductress and a middle-class black
man meet on a New York subway and act out a violent para-
digm of the growing racial tensions in American society.
Crowley introduced audiences to the perspective and experience of another minority in *The Boys in the Band* (1968), presenting a group of homosexual men adjusting with varying de-
grees of success to guilt, loneliness and social opprobrium.

45

Meanwhile, the Phoenix Theatre's biggest commercial success came shortly after its move to a smaller theatre in 1961, with Arthur Kopit's *Oh Dad Poor Dad Mama's Hung You in the Closet and I'm Feeling So Sad*, a surrealistic farce about an overpowering mother and her thoroughly cowed son. Jack Richardson's *The Prodigal* (1960) and *Gallows Humor* (1961) and Murray Schisgal's short comedies *The Typists* and *The Tiger* (1962) were also impressive. New playwrights of another sort were the specialty of the American Place Theatre, a company dedicated to allowing established authors from other fields to experiment with dramatic writing. Its first success was with poet Robert Lowell's double bill *The Old Glory* (1964), dramatizations of stories by Melville and Hawthorne. Two scholar-poets followed: Ronald Ribman with *Harry, Noon and Night* (1965) and *The Journey of the Fifth Horse* (1966), and William Alfred with *Hogan's Goat* (1965).

José Quintero continued to have success as a director at the Circle in the Square, which had moved from its original home to another Greenwich Village theatre but retained its trademark arena stage. In 1961 artistic and personal differences with Theodore Mann led Quintero to leave the company, with Mann taking over both artistic and business management; Quintero's final Circle production was the very successful staging of Genêt's *The Balcony*. The best new director of the period was Alan Schneider (b. 1917), who had previously directed some light comedies and melodramas on Broadway and who directed the American premiere of *Waiting for Godot* in 1956. That led to the Off-Broadway production of Beckett's *Endgame*, to the American premieres of each of Beckett's other plays, and to most of Albee's Off-Broadway and Broadway plays. Schneider's special strength lay in giving these new and potentially bewildering works a foundation in solid reality of setting and characterization so that audiences could make the connection between the world of the plays and their own familiar reality. Gene Frankel was a skilled director and teacher with a particular affinity for plays of political and social comment. As director of Genêt's *The Blacks* (1961), he experimented with a rehearsal technique that would become very popular later in the decade, leading his actors through discussions, encounter sessions and improvisations in which they discovered and harnessed their own passions and convictions about the play's racial themes. (This production of *The Blacks* is im-

The Old Glory, by Robert Lowell. Frank Langella, Roscoe Lee Browne (American Place Theatre, 1964). (Photo by Martha Holmes)

portant for another reason: during its 1000-performance run it employed hundreds of black actors, giving experience and exposure that boosted many careers.) After Stuart Vaughan left the New York Shakespeare Festival, Gerald Freedman and Joseph Papp himself continued the work of making Shakespeare come alive for contemporary audiences.

It was during this same period that Off-Broadway also developed a distinctive variant on that Broadway staple, the musical comedy. The success of *The Threepenny Opera* showed that audiences would accept a musical without Broadway's large casts, elaborate production values and full orchestras. But the modest production style had to be an integral part of the show, not a limitation placed on it; the Phoenix Theatre's *The Golden Apple* (1954) and *Once Upon a Mattress* (1959) were really displaced Broadway shows. Closer to the mark was the 1959 Off-Broadway revival of Jerome Kern's 1917 musical *Leave It to Jane*; the production's affectionate and slightly patronizing tone toward its simple story and innocent world underscored a delicateness that would have been buried in a more elaborate staging. In the even more overtly satiric *Little Mary Sunshine* (1959), Rick Besoyan's parody of Nelson Eddy–Jeanette Mac-Donald operettas drew much of its humor from the disparity between its grand passions and the small stage on which they were played. And it would be hard to imagine a more fragile musical than Tom Jones and Harvey Schmidt's *The Fantasticks* (1960), a dreamlike story of lovers overcoming obstacles that were really placed in their way just to encourage their love; yet with its appropriately modest production and its appropriately tiny theatre it has run for twenty years with no sign of stopping. Later Off-Broadway musical successes have generally had the same modest quality: *You're a Good Man, Charlie Brown* (1967), songs and sketches based on the "Peanuts" cartoons; *Your Own Thing* (1968), a mod version of *Twelfth Night*; and *Godspell* (1970), a festive retelling of the Gospel story.

Between 1950 and 1962 Off-Broadway theatres presented close to one thousand productions, of which a third were new American plays. Starting in 1957 there were more theatres in operation and more productions each season Off-Broadway than on. But as the 1960s progressed, Off-Broadway's vitality and creative energy seemed to wane. The dramatic renaissance that the Albee generation had seemed to promise failed to materialize, at least Off-Broadway. Many of the new play-wrights proved unable to follow up on their first successes, while others sought their fortunes elsewhere. Albee, Murray Schisgal, Tom Jones and Harvey Schmidt went to Broadway; Jack Gelber turned to directing; and LeRoi Jones left the the-atre to devote himself to political and social action in the black community. Meanwhile inflation and rising audience expecta-tions made the shoestring operations of the early years no longer viable; in the mid-1960s a production could cost over $25,000 to mount, and Off-Broadway began to feel the hit-or-flop pressures of Broadway as producers became more cau-tious and more concerned with attracting audiences. Edward Albee spoke for those who wanted to believe things hadn't changed when he said in 1964,

> Off-Broadway is a losing economic proposition. The actors are not in it for money. The producers are not in it for money. The playwright is not in it for money. The off-Broadway theater simply has to be subsidized by the actors, the producers, the playwrights, the directors.[12]

But a year later his own producers were forced to admit they could find no new plays they could risk staging, and marked time with a season of revivals of their previous successes.

Two of the four major companies from Off-Broadway's first period were in apparent decline. The Living Theatre spent the mid-1960s in Europe developing a new style and repertoire. The Phoenix Theatre, constantly beset by financial problems and unable to support itself even in its new small theatre, withdrew from Off-Broadway production and served as host-producer for the APA. The Circle in the Square was perhaps the least affected; having established a place and an audience for itself as the home of sensitively staged revivals and classics, it had successful runs with such plays as Webster's *The White Devil* and O'Neill's *A Moon for the Misbegotten*. A 1969 Circle production drew attention to a new relationship between Broadway and Off-Broadway: Jules Feiffer's *Little Murders*, which had failed on Broadway only a year earlier, was success-fully reconceived and redirected for the smaller Circle theatre. As the earlier revivals of Williams and O'Neill had suggested, Off-Broadway's intimacy, sensitivity and more sophisticated audience could provide a congenial home for plays that had been meant for Broadway.

49

Delacorte Theater, Central Park. (Courtesy of the New York Shakespeare Festival)

Alone among the older companies, the New York Shakespeare Festival actually grew and flourished through the decade. Joseph Papp, using all his skills as salesman, politician and arm-twister, successfully cajoled money and support from the city, the foundations and a loyal group of private donors. In 1962 the Delacorte Theater in Central Park opened; in 1964 a bus-and-truck company began to tour New York's other parks and neighborhoods; and in 1966 Papp realized his dream of a permanent year-round theatre. Private donations enabled the Festival to buy the landmark Astor Library building in downtown Manhattan and convert it into the Public Theater, with three playing spaces and a film theatre. (In 1971 Papp would pull off an even greater coup by convincing the city to buy the building from him and lease it back for a dollar a year, thus replenishing the Festival's coffers and freeing it from the enormous mortgage expenses.) Meanwhile, the Festival's summer Shakespeare seasons maintained a remarkably high quality, with such successes as *The Merchant of Venice* with George C. Scott as Shylock in 1963 and *Othello* with James Earl Jones in 1964. The first production at the Public Theater was a new rock musical called *Hair* which, in a revised version, would become the first of many Festival shows to move to Broadway and national success. The highlight of the Public's second season was Charles Gordone's *No Place To Be Somebody*, the first Off-Broadway play to win the Pulitzer Prize.

Gordone's play, a loosely structured picture of growing frustration and anger among the patrons of a Harlem bar, was part of one of the significant developments of this period in Off-Broadway's history: the appearance and growth of black American theatre and drama. The civil rights and black power movements and the example of LeRoi Jones led a number of black writers and performers to turn to the theatre as a platform for self-expression. And although Off-Broadway's audience remained predominantly white, it was liberal and sympathetic, and hungry for new plays. The work of the black dramatists ranged from simple agitprop pieces to poetic reveries, spiritual-based musicals to absurdist farces. Few of the writers had mastered all the technical requirements of structure and characterization, but the best were able to overcome their awkwardness through the power of their moral commitment or the freshness of their vision. Among the successes were *Ceremonies in Dark Old Men* (1969), Lonnie Elder's quietly tragic study of the generation of urban blacks who were too old and tired to dream of revolution, and Douglas Turner Ward's *Day of Absence* (1966), in which black actors in whiteface parodied the reactions of a southern town on the day all the blacks disappeared. In 1968 Ward and actor Robert Hooks founded the Negro Ensemble Company, which was soon followed by the Black Theater Workshop and the New Lafayette Theater. All maintained high standards of play selection and production, encouraging a slowly growing black audience while helping black writers communicate with concerned whites.

Other social forces of the late 1960s were also reflected Off-Broadway, which was often quicker to respond than more commercial art forms. The antiwar movement found voice in several plays, among them Megan Terry's *Viet Rock* (1966) and Barbara Garson's *MacBird!* (1967), which presented President Lyndon Johnson as Shakespeare's murderous Macbeth. Broader criticism of American society was expressed in Jean-Claude van Itallie's *America Hurrah* (1966) and in the group creations with which the Living Theatre toured the country in 1968 and 1969, openly calling for social and political revolution. There was a lighter side as well: 1968 became the year of the nudes and the dirty words as Off-Broadway playwrights and directors topped each other in breaking the taboos of censorship and taste.

The outlines of the entire American theatre were changing during this period, inspired and instigated to a great extent by Off-Broadway's successful challenge to the Broadway monopoly in the 1950's. Repertory companies and resident theatres had been established all over the country, and some of them had generated satellite "Off-Broadways" of their own. Even in New York City, something calling itself Off Off-Broadway had appeared in the early 1960s, and this second generation of shoestring theatres housed in cabarets, coffeehouses and churches was taking over Off-Broadway's former role as the home of the avant-garde.

Meanwhile, the economic pressures that led Off-Broadway producers to caution and greater commercial considerations in the 1960s only grew worse in the 1970s, when the costs of producing a play or musical Off-Broadway reached the levels of Broadway production twenty years earlier. Critic Robert

Brustein had been somewhat premature in 1961 when he complained that

> *Accompanying [Off-Broadway's] heightened prestige . . . has come a growing reluctance to take chances. . . . The rise in ticket prices and production costs, the employment of high salaried actors from the commercial stage, the burgeoning of new high-rent theaters, the marked increase in press-agentry and advertising—all these tokens, along with a general decline in the quality of off Broadway fare, suggest that powerful economic pressures are putting the squeeze on off Broadway's aesthetic freedom.*[13]

But there is no doubt that the more conservative Otis L. Guernsey, Jr. was a bit overdue in coming to the same conclusion twelve years later:

> *Shrinking straight-play and expanding musical volume; reluctance to experiment, with a consequently lower level of invention; rising production costs and substantial ticket prices. . . . Off Broadway appears to be changing from a free-swinging adventure into some sort of mini-commercial theater, inheriting all the problems which have for so long burdened Broadway.*[14]

Off-Broadway's fate in the 1970s was so tightly tied up with those of Broadway and Off Off-Broadway that it can best be discussed with them in Chapters 4 and 5. Two points do need to be made here. First, Off-Broadway did continue to exist and function as a significant part of the New York City theatre. And second, if Off-Broadway came to resemble Broadway more and more, as Guernsey suggested, much of that resemblance was caused by the fact that Broadway had become more like it. By 1970 Albee, Kopit and Schisgal had become Broadway writers, as had Pinter, Brecht and Ionesco. José Quintero and Alan Schneider were Broadway directors, and *Hair* and three seasons of the APA–Phoenix had played uptown. In the 1970s, transfers from Off-Broadway to Broadway became even more frequent, with the New York Shakespeare Festival in particular becoming the source of some of Broadway's biggest commercial and critical successes. Meanwhile, the explosion of theatrical activity around the country produced dozens of new plays and new playwrights that came to New York to be staged on, Off- and Off Off-Broadway almost interchangeably. It was not so much that Off-Broadway, having had its experimental fling, had retreated back into the theatrical mainstream. Rather, that mainstream had been altered and expanded so that artists and sensibilities that had begun Off-Broadway now made up a significant part of it.

Notes

1. T. Edward Hambleton and Norris Houghton, "Phoenix on the Wing," *Theatre Arts* 38 (November 1954): 29.

2. Joseph Papp, as quoted in "Brooklyn's Gift to the Bard," *Theatre Arts* 42 (January 1958): 11.

3. Julian Beck and Judith Malina, typescript in the Billy Rose Theatre Collection, New York Public Library.

4. José Quintero, *If You Don't Dance They Beat You* (Boston: Little, Brown, 1974), p. 79.

5. Quintero, pp. 215–64.

6. Julian Beck, "Why Vanguard?" *New York Times*, 22 March 1959, Sec. 2, p. 3.

7. Hambleton and Houghton, p. 94.

8. Stuart W. Little, *Off-Broadway* (New York: Dell Publishing Company, 1974), p. 153.

9. Papp, p. 11.

10. Robert Brustein, *Seasons of Discontent* (New York: Simon & Schuster, 1967), p. 43.

11. Little, p. 216.

12. Edward Albee, as quoted in Little, p. 229.

13. Brustein, pp. 42–43.

14. Otis L. Guernsey, Jr., *The Best Plays of 1972–1973* (New York: Dodd, Mead, 1973), pp. 25–27.

Regional Theatre

The Civic Light Opera Companies of Los Angeles and San Francisco were formed to produce annual seasons of Viennese operetta. But around 1950 they found themselves in a new role, as coproducers and in essence underwriters of the national companies of such Broadway musicals as *Where's Charley?* and *Guys and Dolls.* Most Broadway successes had one or more touring companies during or after their New York run, but it was generally agreed that there were few profitable cities west of Chicago, and producers of elaborate and expensive shows were reluctant to make a long western trip just to play two stops in California. So the California organizations had to guarantee the New York producers' profits and occasionally make up their losses to be included in the national tours. For much the same reason many touring dramas and comedies never reached the West Coast either, as the original producers found it safer to license local restagings. For example, while some cities elsewhere in the country were visited by the New York-based touring company of *The Cocktail Party* in 1951, Californians saw a production that originated at the La Jolla Playhouse.

About the same time the phenomenon of summer stock was booming. Summer theatres, amateur and professional, had existed since the Elitch Gardens in Denver started offering plays in 1890. The traditionally slow season in New York led actors and producers to follow vacationing audiences to their rural retreats and resort towns, and by the summer of 1949 there were at least 125 professional repertory companies and about the same number of amateur groups performing in barns, tents, resort hotels and theatres. The professional companies alone presented more than 450 plays, usually for one- or two-week runs, and frequently with established Broadway and Hollywood stars in the leading roles.

But a fifth of those 250 theatres were in New York State, and almost all the rest were in New Jersey, Pennsylvania and the New England states—i.e., where the Broadway audience went for the summer. Except for a couple of Shakespeare festivals and an occasional stab at Chekhov or Restoration comedy, the summer stock seasons were made up almost entirely of recent Broadway hits. In 1949 twenty-six professional theatres offered *The Heiress*, twenty-one did *John Loves Mary*, and so on. There were about a hundred new plays, but all were pre-Broadway tryouts looking for producers or underwritten by Broadway producers; the Theatre Guild, for example, frequently used the Country Playhouse in Westport, Connecticut, to test new scripts before investing in full productions. (Only four of the one hundred new plays in 1949 actually got to Broadway, and only one—*Come Back, Little Sheba*—succeeded, a typical ratio for the period.) Most of the stock companies were formed in New York with New York actors, and many were managed from there. And most of the big stars appeared in only one play all summer, arriving at a theatre in time for a quick run-through with a local cast that had rehearsed without them, playing a week, and then moving on to another theatre offering the same play. A few years later, in a repetition of the nineteenth-century pattern, this system was replaced by complete touring casts, eliminating the need for many local companies and turning local producers into little more than landlords.

These two examples—the California productions and the summer stock companies—demonstrate the total domination of the professional American theatre by Broadway at midcentury. There was theatre outside Manhattan, but it was either Broadway-based, Broadway-bound or a Broadway surrogate. There were hundreds of theatres and, at peak season, thousands of actors at work in America. But there was no real American theatre independent of New York. When a national theatre appeared—or, rather, when a number of companies

Margo Jones. (Photo by Lucas-Pritchard; courtesy of the Billy Rose Theatre Collection, The New York Public Library at Lincoln Center. Astor, Lenox and Tilden Foundations.)

began to establish independent identities around the country—the roots were not in Broadway or its professional outposts, but in the amateur community theatre movement.

Margo Jones (1913–1955) was a talented and dedicated director who had worked with the Pasadena Playhouse and the Ojai, California, Community Players before founding the Houston Community Players in 1936. After several years in Houston, she concluded that really high quality productions required the rehearsal and preparation time that only a professional company could afford, and chose Dallas as a city likely to support such a company. She spent most of the 1940s organizing what was to become Theatre '47 (later Theatre '48, and so on), the first nonprofit professional resident repertory theatre in America.

The significance of Theatre '47 does not merely lie in the fact that it was first; Jones's accomplishments and her messianic zeal directly influenced many of the theatres that followed. Although she herself thought that her advocacy of theatre-in-the-round staging was her biggest contribution, it was really her vision and her call to action, as expressed in her book *Theatre-in-the-Round*:

> *The dream of all serious theatre people in the United States in the middle of our twentieth century is the establishment of a national*

57

*theatre. . . . What our country needs today, theatrically speak-
ing, is a resident professional theatre in every city with a population of over one hundred thousand. . . . Every town in America
wants theatre! It is the duty and business of a capable theatre
person to go into the communities of this country and create fine
theatres.*[1]

Theatre-in-the-Round became, in Joseph Wesley Zeigler's
words, "the nearest thing to a bible in the regional theatre
world,"[2] and Jones's accomplishments, public statements and
willingness to counsel and encourage others made Theatre '47
a model for other companies in its organization and operation.
In purely practical terms, it is likely that Margo Jones's decision to incorporate her theatre as a nonprofit organization had
the most far-reaching effects. She recognized that a resident
repertory company was too expensive an operation to support
itself entirely through the box office; a nonprofit corporation,
with a board of directors made up of civic and social leaders,
not only encouraged donations but also involved the community in the theatre's future. Virtually every subsequent regional theatre has chosen nonprofit status; and the influx of
private, foundation and government donations has changed
the entire financial set-up of the American theatre.

Other pattern-setting elements were the adoption of a found
space for the actual playhouse, in this case a building on the
State Fairgrounds that was vacant most of the year, and the
establishment of a permanent organization with a professional
staff and resident professional company. For her repertoire
Jones deliberately turned her back on the light Broadway
hand-me-downs that were the staples of amateur companies,
and committed herself to classics (Ibsen, Chekhov, Shakespeare) and new plays (the premieres of Tennessee Williams's
Summer and Smoke and an early version of William Inge's *Dark
at the Top of the Stairs* in the first season). Audiences were
encouraged to subscribe for an entire season, as much to
cement their commitment to the theatre as to provide working
capital. Although each season included at least one week of
rotating repertory, the bulk of the schedule was made up of
two- or three-week runs of each play in turn. (Actual rotating
repertory—that is, a different play each night—is expensive
and very rare in American resident theatre, and even those
companies with "Repertory" in their titles generally schedule

Nina Vance. (Courtesy of the Alley Theatre)

a sequence of continuing runs.) Finally, although Jones acknowledged that the jobs of managing director and artistic director were ideally separate, she filled both roles in her theatre. This proved unfortunate for the Dallas company, which disbanded soon after her untimely death in 1955, but as Stephen Langley warned in a guidebook on production, "It is important to note that every significant resident theatre was founded and operated by a single if not singular personality who could easily qualify as 'dynamic.' "[3]

Two such figures appeared on the scene almost immediately. In 1947 Nina Vance (1915–1980) formed an amateur company in Houston, where Jones's Community Players had become inactive. Two years later she moved from her rented dance studio to a converted factory reached through a back alley, where the Alley Theatre's seasons of Williams, Miller, O'Neill and light comedies inspired enthusiastic community support. This, along with the urging of Margo Jones, encouraged Vance to hire occasional professional guest actors and then, in 1954, to convert the Alley to a fully professional company. (The operative date for such changes in generally when a company "goes Equity," that is, when its actors sign contracts approved by Actors' Equity, the performers' union.

Zelda Fichandler.
(Photo by Tess Steinkolk)

There are some non-Equity professional theatres, and many amateur companies that eventually go Equity pass through a preliminary stage in which amateurs work alongside professionals or actors are paid less than the union minimum.) Meanwhile, in 1950 Zelda Fichandler (b. 1924) formed the amateur Arena Stage in a converted movie house in Washington, D. C., and after one seventeen-play season also made the leap to professional status. Both companies flourished in the years that followed, moving to larger homes, doubling and redoubling their subscription bases and, in the 1960s, building multimillion-dollar theatre buildings to house their expanded activities.

What might be called the Alley-Arena model—the formation under the direction of a charismatic leader of an amateur company that graduates to professional status—was repeated in several other cities. Mack Scism founded the amateur Mummers Theatre in Oklahoma City in 1949 and led it as it grew from a summer tent company producing comic nineteenth-century melodramas to a year-round community theatre in the 1950s and to a professional repertory company in the 1960s. Herbert Blau and Jules Irving began their Actor's Workshop in a San Francisco loft in 1952 and went Equity in 1955; they quickly gained a national reputaton for innovative productions and an adventurous repertoire built around such authors as Brecht, Beckett and Pinter. George Touliatos began the amateur Front Street Theatre in a Memphis hotel ballroom in 1957 and progressed to professional status in 1959.

The example of such ventures inspired other amateur companies to transform themselves into professional theatres, in what might be called the Cleveland Play House model. The Play House, one of the oldest community theatres in America, had had a professional executive director and business staff since the 1920s but had retained its amateur status even as its activities expanded to include an annual summer Shakespeare festival; it finally made the change in 1958. Similarly, the Studio Arena Theatre in Buffalo, New York, begun as an acting school and amateur company in 1927, went Equity in 1965. Theatre Atlanta was formed in 1957 through the merger of several older amateur groups, hired a professional managing director in 1965, and became a professional company in 1966. The Goodman Theatre, an acting school and community theatre associated with Chicago's Art Institute since 1925, formed a professional repertory company in 1969; the company stayed on even after the acting school split away to join a local university. Two theatres that began as professional stock companies (i.e., by booking individually cast productions, frequently with guest stars) in the 1950s reorganized themselves as nonprofit repertory theatres in the 1960s: the Fred Miller Theatre, later the Milwaukee Rep; and the Charles Playhouse in Boston.

A third group of regional theatres were born full-grown in a pattern most glamorously exemplified by the Tyrone Guthrie Theater in Minneapolis. In 1959 three theatre professionals—world-famous director Guthrie (1900–1971), Broadway producer Oliver Rea (b. 1923) and stage manager Peter Zeisler (b. 1923)—decided that the next career challenge they wanted to face was the creation of a professional repertory company. As associates of theirs later admitted, "In the beginning, at least,

Tyrone Guthrie. (Courtesy of the Tyrone Guthrie Theater)

theirs was not an attempt to build a theatre to fit and serve a particular community, but to find a community that would fit and serve a particular theatre—Guthrie's theatre."[4] They considered several cities and chose Minneapolis as much because it was the farthest removed from other theatre centers as for any other reason, and so impressed civic and community leaders with their plans that the 2.25 million-dollar Tyrone Guthrie Theater was built for them. In 1963 a star-filled company directed by Guthrie began its first season and almost overnight gave the entire regional theatre movement what Zeigler called "enhanced legitimacy and new attention:"

> *The emergence of The Guthrie Theater was [a] major turning point of the regional theatre revolution because it further legitimized the movement and gave it national weight. It gave hope to all regional theatres that they too could become known on a national level, that the* Times *might soon cover their opening nights, and that actors like Hume Cronyn and Jessica Tandy might soon set aside a season for them.*[5]

The Guthrie was not immune to the financial and audience-building problems that beset less famous companies, but it remained one of the strongest and most prestigious in the country. On a somewhat more modest scale, several other energetic individuals created full-grown theatres in the 1960s: actor-director Ellis Rabb formed the touring Association of Performing Artists in 1960; Smith College professor Jacques Cartier founded the professional Hartford Stage Company in 1964; and Yale Drama School students Harlan Kleiman and Jon Jory opened New Haven's Long Wharf Theatre in 1965.

A variant on this pattern came with the spread of university-based professional theatres. Colleges and universities have long served as cultural centers in many parts of the country; and as the regional theatre movement grew, some schools created professional acting companies to supplement their theatre teaching and to serve their communities. The Dallas Theater Center was an outgrowth of a Baylor College program in 1959 and was later associated with Trinity University; the Syracuse Repertory Theatre, begun as a Syracuse University student program in 1961, evolved into a professional company in 1966; and the Yale Repertory Theatre (Yale, 1966), Loretto-Hilton Center (Webster College, St. Louis, 1966) and McCarter Theatre (Princeton, 1972) are among others in this category.

Finally, a number of resident theatres were born by outside *fiat*, as civic groups or government agencies decided that a particular city needed a repertory company and ordered its creation. Although this group included two of the resident theatre's biggest success stories, companies in this category (which might be called the Lincoln Center model in honor of its most spectacular failure) generally suffered the greatest birth and growing pains, in part from the absence of the highly-motivated leaders typical of other theatres and in part from the proprietary instincts of the founding bodies. As John Glore pointed out about the Seattle Repertory Theatre,

> *It is significant that the theater was first conceived by the citizenry; and their committee carried the embryonic idea through to its realization. From the beginning then, the citizens rightly held the belief that SRT was their child and must answer to them. . . . This, in part, accounts for SRT's somewhat erratic history.*[6]

The Seattle Rep was brought into being by a local committee in 1963, to make use of a theatre building left over from the

William Ball, right, American Conservatory Theatre director, rehearsing *Cyrano* with Paul Shenar. (Photo by Hank Kranzler)

Seattle World's Fair. Stuart Vaughan, who had led the Phoenix Theatre during its repertory company period, was hired as artistic director but was fired after two seasons as a result of artistic differences with the board of directors. A similar fate befell André Gregory, hired to direct the new Theatre of the Living Arts in Philadelphia in 1965. As he explained later, "The Board and I were both working to create a theatre in Philadelphia. The difficulty was that we were trying to create two different kinds of theatre."[7] Gregory's theatre featured imaginative productions of Beckett, Anouilh and Rochelle Owens; the Board and the Philadelphia audiences evidently wanted *Room Service* and *The Time of Your Life* (which Gregory also staged). Gregory was fired and the theatre put in the hands of a more conservative director.

Also in 1965, William Ball was hired by the board of the Pittsburgh Playhouse when that veteran amateur theatre chose to start afresh as a professional company rather than follow the Cleveland model. Ball had long dreamed of a combination theatre and conservatory in which professional actors could continue to study their craft while performing, and the company he created for Pittsburgh was the American Conservatory Theatre. His first season of Albee, Pirandello, Shakespeare, Moliere and the like was evidently too much of a contrast to the Playhouse's past menu of Broadway comedies, and Ball was dismissed within a year. And while the Seattle Repertory Theatre survived its growing pains, the Pittsburgh Playhouse and Theatre of the Living Arts did not; one lapsed back into amateur status and Broadway hand-me-downs, and the other went bankrupt.

Meanwhile, in one of the success stories of this category, William Ball's American Conservatory Theatre spent 1966 in a critically successful tour of the country that resulted in invitations to settle in Chicago and San Francisco. For a while ACT considered spending half the year in each city, but fundraising was more successful in San Francisco, and the company opened there in 1967. A couple of overly ambitious seasons threatened to sink the new theatre, but some belt-tightening got it through the shaky period and it went on to become one of the most active and prosperous resident repertory companies in the country.

The Repertory Theatre New Orleans and the Inner City Repertory Company in Los Angeles were created in 1966 by the federal Office of Education and the National Endowment for the Arts to perform classic plays for students bused in from area high schools and, incidently, for paying adult audiences. Both companies had to deal with interference and censorship by local school boards as well as the inherent difficulty of satisfying the disparate tastes and needs of their student and adult audiences. Without a local base of support, the New Orleans theatre died with the end of its federal funding, and the Inner City Rep survived in modified form on the government and foundation grants for its associated community cultural center. (A third theatre in this federal project, Trinity Square Repertory Company in Providence, Rhode Island, was already functioning as a community theatre and was helped in its advancement to professional status by the government grant; it survived and flourished afterward.)

Curiously, one of the biggest successes in the resident theatre movement and its greatest disaster have similar backgrounds: both were created externally to fill massive multimillion-dollar arts centers. But the Center Theatre Group flourished in Los Angeles's Music Center, while the Repertory Theater of Lincoln Center in New York City collapsed under its own weight three separate times. This makes them worthy of special analysis.

The Los Angeles Music Center is one of the many downtown arts centers built in the culture revival and urban renewal fervor of the 1960s. It consists of three theatres: the 3250 seat Dorothy Chandler Pavilion, home of the Los Angeles Philharmonic and the Light Opera Company; and the 2100-seat Ahmanson Theatre and 742-seat arena-stage Mark Taper Forum, both built to be operated by a resident play-producing organization. One key to the Center's success, undoubtedly, is that it did not attempt to create a new theatre company, but rather adopted and expanded one that had already developed an identity and an audience. The Theatre Group, as it was then called, was formed in 1959 in a loose alliance with the University of California in Los Angeles. Led first by John Houseman and then by Gordon Davidson, it did not employ a permanent company, but drew on the pool of Hollywood-based actors eager to do stage work. Despite its challenging repertoire of classic and contemporary plays and its relative poverty and inaccessibility—the Group received no subsidy from UCLA but was merely allowed to borrow whatever campus theatre,

Gordon Davidson.
(Courtesy of the Mark Taper Forum)

The Music Center of the County of Los Angeles. From top, Ahmanson Theatre, Mark Taper Forum, Dorothy Chandler Pavilion. (Courtesy of the Mark Taper Forum)

lecture hall or classroom was not being used by university groups on a given date—the Theatre Group built up a loyal following. When Davidson (b. 1933) was invited to move his operation downtown in 1967 he brought along a subscription base of 11,000 and a reputation that attracted 20,000 more.

The Center Theatre Group's activities were divided between its two theatres. At the Mark Taper Forum Davidson continued to do uncompromisingly challenging and provocative plays. with a special emphasis on American premieres such as John Whiting's *The Devils* (1967) and Heiner Kipphardt's *In the Mat-*

The Mark Taper Forum. (Courtesy of the Mark Taper Forum)

ter of J. Robert Oppenheimer (1968), and world premieres such as Conor Cruise O'Brien's *Murderous Angels* (1970). An integral part of the Taper program was New Theatre for Now, workshop productions of new American plays, some of which graduated into the regular season. New Theatre for Now's alumni list challenges that of the Barr-Wilder-Albee Playwrights Unit in New York: John Guare, Oliver Hailey, Israel Horovitz, Adrienne Kennedy, Terrence McNally, Leonard Melfi, Robert Patrick, Lanford Wilson.

The larger Ahmanson Theatre hosted visiting productions and staged more conventional works, many of them essentially Broadway tryouts. In a variant on the old use of summer stock to test plays, Ahmanson productions would be offered to New York producers or coproduced with them. The New York producer got the opportunity to test the project with the Center Theatre Group bearing or sharing the initial expense, while the Group was able to mount productions and attract stars it might otherwise not have been able to afford, and to participate in the profits, if any, from the New York run. The Center Theatre Group's first Ahmanson production in 1967 was the American premiere of Eugene O'Neill's posthumous *More Stately Mansions*, directed by José Quintero and starring Ingrid Bergman and Colleen Dewhurst. In the years that followed it would also send such plays as Alan Ayckbourn's *The Norman Conquests* (1975) and Neil Simon's *California Suite* (1976) on to New York.

The first of the great urban renewal arts centers of the 1960s was Lincoln Center for the Performing Arts, about a mile north of the Broadway theatre district in New York. With homes for the Metropolitan Opera, the New York Philharmonic, the New York City Opera and Ballet companies, the Juilliard School and the New York Public Library's performing arts collection, all it needed was a resident theatre company. The Lincoln Center Board of Directors hired experienced Broadway producer Robert Whitehead and director Elia Kazan to form and direct such a company; and they in turn recruited director-critic Harold Clurman, playwright Arthur Miller and an acting company led by Hal Holbrook, Ralph Meeker, David Wayne and Jason Robards, Jr. Since the 1100-seat Vivian Beaumont Theater (with a smaller studio theatre in its basement) that was to be its home was not completed, the Repertory Theater of Lincoln Center played its first two seasons

Lincoln Center. Clockwise from lower left: New York State Theater, Metropolitan Opera House, Vivian Beaumont Theater, Juilliard School, Avery Fisher Hall. (Courtesy of the New York Convention & Visitors Bureau)

Vivian Beaumont Theater. (Photo by Ezra Stoller © ESTO)

(1964–1965) in a temporary theatre especially built for it in Greenwich Village. The opening production was Miller's new *After the Fall*, directed by Kazan. It was followed by O'Neill's *Marco Millions*, directed by José Quintero; S. N. Behrman's new comedy *But For Whom Charlie*, directed by Kazan; Middleton's *The Changeling*, also directed by Kazan; *Incident at Vichy*, another new Miller play, directed by Clurman; and William Ball's production of *Tartuffe*.

Clearly, this was a high-powered operation, involving artists of established reputation and talent. It was also a disaster, with only *After the Fall* achieving any critical and popular success. Zeigler reconstructs the thinking of the Lincoln Center Board of Directors:

> *The Repertory Theatre of Lincoln Center in this first phase had been an attempt to form a National Theatre out of the best of Broadway, and it failed. If talents like Kazan's and Whitehead's could not create a National Theatre, none from Broadway could—and therefore the talent for the job would have to come from beyond.*[8]

In December 1964 the Board fired Whitehead, leading Kazan, Miller and Clurman to resign in protest. Herbert Blau and Jules Irving of the Actor's Workshop in San Francisco were hired to create a new company and start all over for the Beaumont's opening in 1965. Their first New York season was a challenging and adventurous one: *Danton's Death*, *The Country Wife*, *The Condemned of Altona* and *The Caucasian Chalk Circle*. It was also a critical and box office flop. After an equally unsuccessful second season Blau resigned in despair, leaving Irving to struggle on for five more years, during which the repertory company was disbanded and individually cast productions, generally of such safe classics as Shaw's *St. Joan*, were offered to shrinking audiences and growing deficits. By the end of the decade the Beaumont was losing $800,000 a year, and in 1971 the Lincoln Center Board seriously considered a proposal to turn the building into a complex of movie theatres. In 1972 Irving finally gave up. (The curse that haunted the Beaumont had meanwhile cast its spell across the country: without Blau and Irving the Actor's Workshop disbanded in 1966.)

In 1973 the Board of Directors called in the one man in the country who seemed likely to be able to defy the curse, and the

Beaumont Theater became part of Joseph Papp's New York Shakespeare Festival empire. Papp announced a policy of producing new plays in the main theatre and a year-round Shakespeare festival in the smaller house, but after two money-losing years he dropped the Shakespeare, moved the new plays downstairs and offered a series of revivals and classics in the main theatre. After two more years he too quit, complaining that the Beaumont's losses were draining the New York Shakespeare Festival's resources and threatening its other operations. The Beaumont Theater remained dark until the end of the decade, when another management began.

There is no single reason why the theatre in Los Angeles succeeded and the one in New York failed, but the contributing factors illuminate the problems and triumphs of other resident theatres. Putting aside individual personalities and personality clashes, which no doubt contributed, the fact that Lincoln Center tried to create a mature repertory company out of thin air while Los Angeles allowed a going concern to flourish under its sponsorship is certainly an important difference. The Center Theatre Group began with at least some of its growing pains behind it, while Lincoln Center's first directors had to learn how to operate a repertory theatre as they went along; for example, part of their difficulty in the first two seasons arose from the basic error of choosing an acting company primarily to meet the needs of *After the Fall* and then having to squeeze them into the other plays.

The Center Theatre Group also had an artistic identity and a core audience from the start, and its three-tier structure (conventional plays in the Ahmanson, more adventurous productions in the Taper and new plays in the Monday night workshops) allowed audiences with different tastes to come with some idea of the sort of theatrical experience they were going to have. The Lincoln Center operation changed leadership, styles and repertoires every few years in its desperate attempt to find something that worked, and never gave a loyal audience time to find it. (Identity problems of this sort threatened the Tyrone Guthrie Theater as well; when the novelty of the new building wore off and the star-studded first company left, subscriptions fell radically and the management had to work hard to build an audience that would come to a resident company for its own sake.)

More significantly, the Center Theatre Group met a real

need that the Lincoln Center theatre did not. By 1967 Los Angeles was theatre-hungry and the Center Theatre Group was to a great extent the only game in town. Audiences, financial supporters and even critics were primed to like it and to want it to succeed. In a very real sense the Repertory Theater of Lincoln Center had no reason for existing; while it would have been nice, in theory, for New York City to have a major repertory company, it filled no real audience need. *After the Fall* certainly would have found a Broadway producer, and *But For Whom Charlie* was in fact scheduled for Broadway production by Whitehead, with Kazan directing, and was put into the Lincoln Center schedule instead. Many of Blau and Irving's plays would eventually have been done Off-Broadway, and Papp's Beaumont seasons were admittedly extensions of the work he was doing elsewhere in the city. Audiences came to the Metropolitan Opera in Lincoln Center because the old Opera House had been torn down, but there was no built-in reason to come to the Beaumont. The successful resident theatres around America were those that satisfied an audience hunger for good theatre; where that hunger didn't exist (in Pittsburgh, for example), simply creating a theatre didn't create an audience. (In contrast, the fact that William Ball's ACT arrived in San Francisco the year after the Actor's Workshop died undoubtedly contributed to its enthusiastic welcome.)

Perhaps the biggest cause of Lincoln Center's repeated failures was the public perception of the theatre and its offerings. When it opened in the mid-1960s New York City had two clearly distinct theatrical environments, Broadway and Off-Broadway. In its structure and ambitions the Repertory Theater of Lincoln Center may have had more in common with such Off-Broadway operations as the Circle in the Square, but the public and the critics always saw and judged it in Broadway terms. Certainly the backgrounds and offerings of its first directors did little to discourage this identification, and the impressive new Beaumont Theater with its classy neighbors did not inspire the kind of lowered expectations and willingness to experiment that New Yorkers had learned to bring to Off-Broadway. The real curse that haunted the Vivian Beaumont Theater was the smash-hit-or-flop syndrome of the commercial Broadway theatre, where anything less than overwhelming success was total failure. Brooks Atkinson points out the absurdity of measuring Lincoln Center by Broadway standards:

During the 1972–1973 season [Irving's last] the Lincoln Center Repertory Theater lost less than usual. It lost $700,000. Vast sums of money were lost on Broadway on less significant enterprises. . . . For $146,000 less than the cost of the disasterous musical Via Galactica, *the Lincoln Center Repertory Theater put on five productions that attracted audiences for seven months. It cost the Repertory less to subsidize a full season than it cost the commercial theater to stage one intolerable musical.*[9]

The experience of the Papp years illustrates the power of the Beaumont's false image most clearly. The Shakespeare Festival's productions at Lincoln Center were no different in range and style from those at the Public Theater downtown, and any single Beaumont season had about the same proportion of strong and weak plays as a typical Public season. But audiences came to the Public and they came back again even if what they had seen the previous time wasn't any good, because of their faith in and affection for the Festival as a continuing operation. Going to a Festival production at the Beaumont just wasn't the same thing; it was like going to Broadway, and audiences demanded perfection every time out. No repertory theatre can produce equally high quality work in every production every season, and this is something that Public Theater audiences and audiences in other cities either sensed from the start or came to understand. Audiences who understand this are committed to theatre as an ongoing part of their lives rather than as isolated distractions; and that understanding and commitment, never achieved at Lincoln Center, gave the resident theatre movement its vitality and significance.

Not all of the regional theatres born in the 1950s and 1960s survived. The Theatre of the Living Arts, the Pittsburgh Playhouse, the Charles Playhouse, the Front Street Theatre, the Repertory Theatre New Orleans and some others fell victim to financial pressures, personality clashes or the simple fact that their cities were just not ready to support a resident theatre. Still, the blossoming of professional regional theatre activity in the three decades following Margo Jones's planting of the seed in Dallas came very close to fulfilling her dream of a national theatre. In 1950 there was Theatre '50. In 1960 there were a dozen professional resident theatres spread across the country. By 1966 there were thirty, and Actors' Equity reported that more actors were employed in resident theatres than in all the Broadway and road companies combined. At the close of the 1970s the League of Resident Theatres had more than sixty members, and the National Endowment for the Arts estimated that there were ten times as many smaller "alternative" theatres around the country. For the first time in the twentieth century the term "American theatre" was not synonymous with "New York City theatre."

Although every resident theatre had unique features resulting from its origins or location, a number of common patterns, many traceable back to Margo Jones and Theatre '47, were evident. The most significant, aside from the geographical spread, was the fact that each theatre was meant to be a permanent institution and not the *ad hoc* producing operation typical of Broadway. This meant continuity and a very different relationship to the audience. The goal of every resident theatre was to become a fact of life in its community—not a special event like the once-a-year appearance of the circus, but a continuing resource to be visited as casually and frequently as the local movie house. To the extent that individual companies have succeeded in achieving this goal they have not only made professional theatre available where it had not been before, but have given it a role in American life that it had not had for a hundred years.

The majority of companies offered their plays in seasons of sequential two- to six-week runs, and some were able to sell 80 or 90 percent of their tickets through season subscriptions. Again an extraordinary change in audience psychology was being generated: in every city thousands of people bought tickets months in advance to plays that did not come bearing the glory of Broadway success or rave reviews—plays, indeed, that the ticket buyers may not even have heard of before. New York and road company audiences went to see particular plays and stars; resident theatre audiences went to the theatre.

The repertoire of a particular resident company reflected the tastes of its artistic director (and, occasionally, of its governing board), the strengths and limits of its actors and physical resources, and the level of sophistication and adventurousness of its audience. The Mark Taper Forum could offer a much

77

less orthodox selection than, say, the Indiana Repertory Theatre; and Edward Albee might be as radical as one company wanted to get, while another considered him as traditional as Arthur Miller. In most cases the theatre felt an obligation to fill in the gaps in its audience's experience of the classics while also introducing it to new works, and the practicalities of attracting and holding ticket buyers required the inclusion of some light and familiar plays in all but the most adventurous repertoires. Generally a season struck a predictable balance between the familiar and the challenging. A typical five- or six-play package was likely to include one Shakespeare play (or, in a more ambitious company, Jonson, Marlowe, Congreve or even a Greek tragedy); one modern European classic (probably Shaw or Chekhov, possibly Ibsen, Gogol or even Pirandello); one major American writer (Williams, Miller, O'Neill, Wilder); one safe crowd-pleaser to reassure those who might be frightened by the prospect of so much culture (a Neil Simon comedy, *Charley's Aunt*, a musical); probably one contemporary and vaguely avant-garde play (Brecht, Beckett, Pinter, Albee); and, increasingly in the 1970s, a new American play, possibly one developed through the theatre's own playwriting workshop.

Finding the proper balance for the local audience was probably an artistic director's greatest challenge. Serious misjudgments in either direction could alienate subscribers and endanger a theatre's survival: the Pittsburgh and Philadelphia theatres died because their repertoires were too adventurous for their audiences, while the Inner City Repertory Company lost many Los Angeles subscribers by capitulating to Board of Education censorship in its first season. In contrast, whatever their original ambitions, both the Seattle Rep and the Studio Arena in Buffalo achieved community acceptance only by acknowledging the limits of their audiences' adventurousness and retreating to conservative repertoires. (The Seattle Rep was able to have it both ways, by encouraging and assisting the more experimental "alternative" theatres that grew up around it in the 1970s.) Even the experienced Zelda Fichandler could guess wrong. After fourteen years of relatively orthodox classics at the Arena Stage, she decided in 1965 that her audience was ready for less familiar Pinter, Brecht, Anouilh and the like. In two seasons the Arena lost half of its 16,000 subscribers, and quickly returned to a menu of *Macbeth* and *The*

Inspector General. (To be fair to the Washington audience, within the next few years it was ready to support such challenges as Arthur Kopit's *Indians*.)

In addition to the regular season, most theatres offered such special projects as holiday shows, children's theatre, touring productions, student performances and apprentice or training programs—operations that not only attracted new audiences and brought in additional funds but also encouraged a community perception of the theatre as a permanent service resource (The Guthrie Theater sponsored a Boy Scout troop). New play workshops and staged readings became very popular in the 1970s as directors and audiences were drawn to the idea of the resident theatre as source of original plays as well as caretaker of the classics. As companies expanded their activities many opened second and even third playhouses, generally smaller studio theatres for their children's shows or experimental productions.

With occasional exceptions such as the Mark Taper Forum, almost all regional theatres employed resident acting companies, usually for one- or two-year contracts, though in some cases actors might stay with a company for more than a decade. A regional theatre contract offered actors a continuity of employment and an opportunity for growth hitherto virtually unattainable in the American theatre; and while one early fear was that actors could not be lured away from New York and Hollywood, a remarkable number chose to build their careers moving from company to company and developing their skills in a larger variety of roles than they would ever have had occasion to play otherwise. Jane Alexander, René Auberjonois, Robert Foxworth, George Grizzard, Stephen Joyce, Stacy Keach, Frank Langella and Anthony Zerbe are among many whose regional theatre experience helped shape their talents and reputations.

One sign of the regional theatre's growing strength and significance was the number of New York-based artists who became involved in it. Hume Cronyn and Jessica Tandy joined the Guthrie Theater company for its first seasons, and they and other established Broadway actors have played in regional theatres with increasing frequency. Directors Stuart Vaughan and William Ball left promising New York careers to commit themselves to regional companies, while others such as Alan Schneider moved freely between New York and regional assignments; in 1959 Schneider used a Ford Foundation grant to subsidize a year spent directing plays at several regional theatres that could not have afforded his services otherwise. Authors who could easily have found Broadway producers have given their plays to resident companies instead; Paddy Chayefsky's *The Latent Heterosexual* had its first production at the Dallas Theater Center in 1968; Edward Albee gave his *Box-Mao-Box* to the Studio Arena Theatre in the same year; Robert Anderson's *Solitaire/Double Solitaire* began at the Long Wharf in 1971; and Jerome Lawrence and Robert E. Lee have premiered several plays at regional theatres. In 1970, through a program called American Playwrights Theater, Lawrence and Lee's *The Night Thoreau Spent in Jail* was produced concurrently by more than 100 professional and university theatres; the authors happily noted that more people saw that play in one season than had seen their biggest Broadway hits, *Inherit the Wind* and *Mame*, in their total combined runs.

Further evidence of regional theatre's vitality and fertility lies in its original contributions to the American dramatic repertoire. A generation of young American dramatists—Michael Cristofer, Oliver Hailey, Terrence McNally, David Mamet, Sam Shepard and others—was discovered or nurtured by regional companies. Such plays as Arthur Kopit's *Indians*, first done at the Arena in 1969; Preston Jones's "Texas Trilogy" (*The Last Meeting of the Knights of the White Magnolia, Lu Ann Hampton Laverty Oberlander* and *The Oldest Living Graduate*, from the Dallas Theater Center, 1973); Michael Cristofer's *The Shadow Box* (Mark Taper Forum, 1975); David Mamet's *A Life in the Theatre* (Goodman Theatre, 1976) and Christopher Durang's *A History of the American Film* (Hartford Stage Company, 1977) have been staged around the country as frequently as *Hamlet* or *St. Joan*. Regional theatres also introduced Americans to European plays too challenging or risky for commercial producers: the first professional production of Brecht's *Caucasian Chalk Circle* (Arena Stage, 1961), Edward Bond's *Bingo* (Cleveland Play House, 1965), David Storey's *The Changing Room* (Long Wharf, 1972), David Rudkin's *Ashes* (Mark Taper Forum, 1976) and dozens of others.

A final proof that the vital roots of the American theatre were now elsewhere than that square mile of Manhattan was a striking change in the role of Broadway. Instead of being the source of all new plays and productions, New York became

Box-Mao-Box: Lucille Patton, Conrad Yama, William Needles, Jenny Egan (Studio Arena Theatre). (Photo by Sherwin Greenberg, McGranahan & May Inc.)

The Gin Game, by D. L. Coburn. Jessica Tandy, Hume Cronyn (Long Wharf Theatre). (Photo by William B. Carter)

more and more a showcase for work originated someplace else. Most of the plays already mentioned were picked up by New York producers after their regional premieres (as opposed to being conceived of from the start as Broadway try-outs) and given Broadway or Off-Broadway runs. To the list could be added Paul Zindel's *The Effect of Gamma Rays on Man-in-the-Moon Marigolds* (Alley Theatre, 1965), Howard Sackler's *The Great White Hope* (Arena, 1967), the musical *Raisin* (Arena, 1973), David Mamet's *American Buffalo* (Goodman, 1975), David Rabe's *Streamers* (Long Wharf, 1976) and Arthur Kopit's *Wings* (Yale, 1979).

Although many companies were born without theatre buildings and had to follow the lead of the Arena and Alley, playing in converted warehouses and other found spaces, the rapid expansion of the resident theatre movement in the mid-1960s coincided with a period of national economic strength and the era of urban renewal. For a while it seemed as if every city in America was attempting to revitalize its downtown with an arts center of some sort. Lincoln Center in New York, the Los Angeles Music Center and the Kennedy Center in Washington are the best-known products of this flurry of building. Private, government and foundation money also created multimillion-dollar homes for the Alley Theatre, the Arena Stage, the Mummers Theatre and the Milwaukee Rep; indeed, more than 170 theatres and arts centers were built between 1962 and 1969, with more than 60 percent of all private, government and foundation support for the performing arts devoted to construction. Those cities that didn't build new homes for their resident companies at least converted and refurbished older theatres or grand old movie palaces, so the majority of resident companies born during this period soon found themselves in relatively luxurious playing spaces.

The importance of this extensive theatre-building can't be underestimated. A new theatre was a tangible sign of local commitment, an indication that the resident company was seen as a permanent part of the community. It also had direct artistic and economic effects; as a Twentieth Century Fund task force pointed out in 1970, "The largest single controllable factor in the health of the performing arts is the attractiveness, technical adequacy, and financial efficiency of their housing."[10] Aside from the artistic freedom and opportunities a fully equipped theatre provides for an acting company, it has a

The Great White Hope: James Earl Jones (Arena Stage). (Photo by Fletcher Drake)

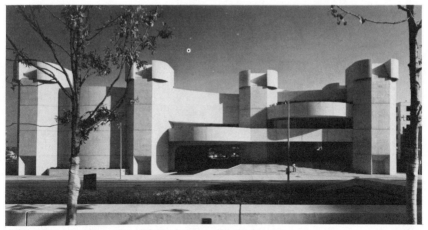

Alley Theatre, Houston. (Photo by Ezra Stoller)

measurable psychological effect on an audience: civic pride, a sense of occasion and simple physical comfort can significantly increase the attractiveness of theatregoing and the pleasure of the experience. While there were certainly other factors involved, it is notable that the Center Theatre Group's subscription base in its first year was almost three times what it had been at UCLA. The Arena Stage was ten years old, with a strong identity and loyal following, when it moved to its new theatre, yet subscriptions jumped 45 percent in the first season there. The Milwaukee Repertory Theatre more than doubled its subscriptions with the move to the Performing Arts Center, and the Tyrone Guthrie Theater—the building itself—was a big drawing card in that company's first season.

In contrast, of course, is the Lincoln Center debacle, though it should be noted that the Center's other components—the opera, ballet, etc.—flourished in the new complex. Considering the urban renewal and arts center bandwagon in general, analysts for the Twentieth Century Fund concluded that

> *Perhaps the most important question to be raised about cultural centers is whether as much thought has been given to the nature of their presentations as to the design of the buildings. One suspects that the planners of some of the centers have not really considered in any detail what should be done with the buildings*

*once they were completed, but have proceeded on the assumption
that quality of performance would somehow take care of itself.[11]*

While the Lincoln Center Repertory Theater was the grandest
and most expensive example of this sort of shortsightedness,
the case of the Oklahoma City Mummers was perhaps the
saddest. An amateur company founded in 1949, the Mummers
became a pet project of the Ford Foundation, which gave the
company almost two million dollars between 1959 and 1970 to
help it make the leap to professional status. But virtually all of
that money, along with an almost equal amount from other
sources, went to the building of a massive (and excellent) new
theatre; when it opened in 1970 Ford and the Mummers were
startled to discover that Oklahoma City, which had supported
its modest little local amateur troupe, didn't really want a
company of professional actors in a big new building. The
professional version of the Mummers folded in a year, leaving
the expensive new theatre vacant. Another version of this
error was the experience of Atlanta, Savannah, Indianapolis,
St. Paul and several other cities that chose to build a single
large auditorium to house symphonies, rock concerts and
touring shows as well as plays, and generally found that
compromise designing made it equally not-quite-adequate for
all its planned uses.

The building boom of the 1960s had another effect on the
American theatre, whose significance has yet to be fully felt.
There are fads in theatre design as in other things, and a
rebellion against the proscenium arch made the three-sided
thrust stage very fashionable at the time that all these buildings were being designed and constructed. As a result some of
the most important theatre buildings in America—the Tyrone
Guthrie, the Mark Taper Forum, the Vivian Beaumont, and the
homes of the Alley Theatre, the Dallas Theater Center, the
Hartford Stage Company, the Long Wharf Theatre, the
Loretto-Hilton Repertory Company, the Studio Arena Theatre
and the Yale Rep, among others—have permanent full or
modified thrust stages, with audiences sitting on three sides of
an open playing area. This is a very flexible arrangement, but
one that poses some problems, particularly with plays written
for proscenium stages. It is possible that directors will eventually find this design as constricting as the proscenium was, or
that a generation of young playwrights exposed primarily to

this arrangement will unconsciously shape their plays to fit it in ways that will raise problems for future directors.

The growth of the resident theatre movement and the spread of vital and fertile theatrical activity independent of New York is clearly the most significant development in the American theatre since 1950. But it has been accompanied— and, in fact, made possible—by a second innovation whose importance may eventually be even greater: the liberation of the American theatre from the marketplace.

The fact is that every regional resident theatre company loses money, and loses big. It is the rare case when box office receipts make up more than 75 percent of a theatre's expenses, and 50 percent is closer to the norm. In 1979, for example, the Arena Stage met only two-thirds of its almost three-million dollar annual budget from ticket sales, even while playing to 91 percent of its capacity; the Alaska Repertory Theatre, selling 81 percent of its tickets, earned about one-third of its expenses; and the Missouri Rep sold 82 percent of its tickets and made two-fifths of its budget.

When that happens on Broadway a show closes and its backers lose their money, just as if they had invested in a company that went bankrupt. In the resident theatres for the most part (Lincoln Center again standing out as one of the striking exceptions), the company happily continues operation, with the 50 or 60 percent being made up by sources who believe that the arts aren't *supposed* to be profitable and who don't expect to be repaid. These modern Medicis count among their number some individuals, such as the benefactors for whom the Ahmanson, Taper, Beaumont and Delacorte buildings were named. But they are led by the major philanthropic foundations and, most astoundingly, by the federal, state and local governments.

The beginnings of subsidized theatre in America came in 1957, when the Ford Foundation tentatively inaugurated its program in the arts. After studying the work of such companies as the Alley, the Arena and the Mummers (all three of which would later become leading beneficiaries of the Foundation), Ford decided that the resident theatre movement was the great hope of the American theatre, and determined to support and encourage its growth. Ford began relatively modestly with travel grants allowing the directors of fledgling companies to visit other theatres to observe their operations, and with student internships in theatre management. To test whether ambitious young actors would be willing to commit themselves to repertory companies, the Foundation under-wrote the payrolls of four theatres—the Arena, Alley, Actor's Workshop and Phoenix—for three seasons beginning in 1959. Evidently satisfied with the experiment, Ford upped the ante radically in 1962 with a total of 6.1 million dollars in grants to nine theatres: the Actor's Studio in New York, the Actor's Workshop, the Alley, the American Shakespeare Festival, the Arena, the Fred Miller Theatre in Milwaukee, the Mummers, the UCLA Theatre Group and the Guthrie Theater. The Alley alone received 2.1 million dollars, half of which was desig-nated for the construction of its new theatre; Ford later gave another 1.4 million to that project. The Mummers, still an amateur company barely out of its summer tent state, got 1.25 million, part of a series of grants that pushed it toward full professional status.

The Ford Foundation's original plan was to stimulate re-gional theatres to self-sufficiency through seed money, but it soon discovered that this was an unreasonable hope. A study commissioned by the Twentieth Century Fund in 1966 reached the conclusion that "performing organizations typically oper-ate under constant financial strain—that their costs almost always exceed their earned income"; and, even more significantly, "Because of the economic structure of the per-forming arts, these financial pressures are here to stay, and there are fundamental reasons for expecting the income gap to widen steadily with the passage of time."[12] Later studies by Ford and by the Rockefeller Brothers Fund reached the same conclusion: a resident theatre company, like a symphony or-chestra or a museum, is by its very nature a money-losing operation. To their credit the foundations did not back down from the responsibility to continue their support; in the decade that followed, six-figure grants from the Ford Foundation be-came almost commonplace. In 1971, for example, Ford gave $365,000 to the American Place Theatre in New York; $320,000 to Baltimore's Center Stage; $240,000 to the Hartford Stage Company; $305,000 to the Seattle Rep; $150,000 to Stage/West in West Springfield, Massachusetts; and $357,000 to the Trinity Square Rep. The APA–Phoenix partnership got $900,000 in 1967; the Arena Stage got $600,000 in 1970; the Guthrie re-ceived $619,000 in 1972; the New York Shakespeare Festival got $1,500,000 in 1973; and San Francisco's ACT got a total of more than four million dollars in various grants. (To put these figures in some perspective, remember that by the mid-1970s a single Broadway musical cost more than a million dollars to produce. About the same time the Arena, on an annual budget of about 2.5 million, produced as many as nine plays in addition to workshops, readings and touring productions.)

Many of these grants were unrestricted gifts to be used by the theatres to make up their deficits and keep themselves in operation. Some went to support specific programs, such as new play workshops, or special projects, such as the construction or renovation of a theatre building; Ford built new theatres for the Alley and the Mummers, and bought and renovated theatres for ACT and the Actors Theatre of Louisville. In the mid-1960s the Foundation helped create several ethnic and minority-oriented theatres, including New York's Negro Ensemble Company, the Free Southern Theater and the Inner City Repertory Company. Another grant program focused on more experimental companies such as Off Off-Broadway's Cafe La Mama.

By 1977 the Ford Foundation had given away more than $35,000,000 to theatre companies throughout the country, and in the process had stimulated further millions in contributions from other sources, since many of its grants required the recipients to raise matching funds elsewhere. In addition Ford spent about $11,000,000 on ancillary grants: underwriting of new play production, support of theatre education, individual travel and study fellowships. In 1961 Ford established the Theatre Communications Group, a national service organization for nonprofit theatres large and small. TCG operates a central casting and personnel service; provides expert assistance in management, fund-raising and subscription sales; and organizes conferences and workshops for its member companies.

Ford has been the largest patron of the noncommercial theatre, but not the only one. The Rockefeller Foundation has provided continuing support to many companies, particularly those dedicated to the production of new American plays and the exploration of unconventional production methods; Rockefeller funded the Center Theatre Group's New Theatre for Now, the Milwaukee Rep's Theatre for Tomorrow and ACT's Plays in Progress programs, among others. The Andrew W. Mellon Foundation, the Rockefeller Brothers Fund and the

89

Twentieth Century Fund have also been active contributors, as have hundreds of smaller foundations, corporations and individuals.

More significantly, public money has also been made available to the theatre. In 1966 Congress created the National Endowment for the Arts with an annual grant budget of 2.5 million dollars; by 1978 that had risen to over 100 million. The Endowment funds music, dance, art and broadcasting projects as well as theatre, but it has still been able to support hundreds of companies and individuals. Some established regional theatres have received sizeable grants ($125,000 to the New York Shakespeare Festival; $117,500 to the Arena; $95,000 to ACT, for example, all in 1971), but the National Endowment's prejudice has been in favor of smaller, developing companies and of theatres and writers producing new plays. The bulk of its giving has been in the $5000 to $25,000 range, allowing a greater breadth and diversity of support than is typical of the private foundations. In addition, many states have formed Councils on the Arts, following the lead of New York, which began offering grants to its artists and art institutions in 1960; and some resident theatres also receive support from state and local boards of education, community development agencies, parks departments and even zoning commissions.

Foundation and government subsidy has even found its way into the Broadway theatre. The Theatre Development Fund was established in 1967 by the Twentieth Century Fund, the Rockefeller Brothers Fund and the National Endowment for the Arts to explore the possibilities of injecting subsidy money into the commercial theatre. It began by buying up blocks of tickets to forthcoming plays of artistic merit but uncertain commercial strength and reselling them at a discount to students and similar groups, thereby encouraging new audiences while giving the productions a financial buffer. TDF takes credit for helping such plays as *The Great White Hope*, *The Changing Room*, *The Hot l Baltimore*, *That Championship Season*, *The Shadow Box*, *Sweeney Todd*, *Wings* and *The Elephant Man* weather their first weeks until they caught on with the general public. In 1973 TDF opened a discount ticket booth in Times Square, where Broadway and Off-Broadway shows that were not sold out offered tickets on the day of performance for half price. Soon the discount booth was selling more than a million tickets a year and helping Broadway hold on to the segment of its audience that rising ticket prices were driving away; TDF estimated that up to three-quarters of its customers would not have bought full-price tickets. TDF also instituted a discount voucher system for Off Off-Broadway theatres, supplying the difference between the voucher price and the full ticket price; a costume rental service for nonprofit theatres; and aid to other cities, notably Boston, Chicago and Minneapolis, in developing their own voucher systems.

Subsidy by government, foundation and private sources has become an established part of the structure of the American theatre, and one whose role will probably grow. This situation is not without its dangers; certainly if the money should suddenly disappear few resident companies could adjust and retrench quickly enough to survive in anything resembling their present form. As the experience of the Mummers and the Repertory Theatre New Orleans showed, money unwisely spent can be even more harmful than lack of funds. Looking back with some pride on its involvement in the performing arts since 1957, the Ford Foundation was forced to admit that it might have done some companies a greater service (and saved itself some money) by guiding them toward greater stability and community acceptance before overwhelming them with massive grants.[13] On a smaller scale, the availability of funds earmarked for a special purpose—board of education grants for student performances, for example, or grants to create playwriting workshops—run the risk of diverting a company from its central purposes or tempting it to overextend itself.

More insidious is the danger that financial support implies some artistic control. Cases of direct artistic interference or censorship by funding agencies have fortunately been rare, although some school boards, for example, have demanded a say in the choice of plays their students would see. But self-censorship is always a possibility; as Martin Gottfried warned in 1967,

> There can be no greater loss to the artist than that of self-reliance. Once he becomes dependent upon outsiders, he can no longer be free. . . . There is a pressure to be inoffensive, an inclination to be sleek, proper and bland.[14]

Gottfried suspected that the foundations consciously planned to influence the theatres they funded, but Joseph Wesley Zeigler, who served as executive director of Ford's Theatre Communications Group, saw a different danger:

91

> *The pervasive power of Ford support tended to homogenize and codify theatres, although the villain in this was not really or directly Ford but rather those theatres which homogenized themselves in hopes of thereby gaining Ford support.[15]*

A resident theatre's artistic director might not even realize that he was choosing a repertoire or production style with an eye toward catering to the tastes or prejudices of a potentially friendly foundation. And Zeigler admitted that even the innocent programs of the Theatre Communications Group had artistic implications:

> *TCG homogenized theatres through its casting service, which prompted the appearance of the same actors in various theatres over the years; through its visitation program, which encouraged artists and managers to think and act alike; and through [ticket sales expert] Danny Newman's perigrinations, which provided promotional tools that looked and worked alike. We helped theatres to become more stable but at a high cost to them—a threatened loss of individuality.[16]*

Zeigler is far too harsh on TCG and Ford. The pool of floating actors, to the extent that there was one, meant a steady supply of experienced and growing performers for each company; and the similarities in bookkeeping and advertising were the results of sharing ideas that worked rather than letting each theatre stumble through its own trial-and-error process. But his underlying fear that financial support inevitably has some artistic effects is valid. Broadway folklore is filled with tales of producers forced to hire the untalented sweethearts or nephews of their financial backers. Nothing as grotesque happens in the subsidized theatre, but an accumulation of small artistic compromises and adjustments could be as stultifying.

Still, whatever the dangers, the extraordinary fact remains that for the first time in the history of the United States the professional theatre has been liberated, at least partially, from the demands of the marketplace. The need to make a profit is no longer the overriding concern of theatre managers, and the artistic freedom this change provides means that resident theatres can fill the two important functions that the commercial theatre has always admitted were beyond its ability: the preservation and continued reexamination of the classics, and the stimulation and support of untried new artists. (It is hardly surprising that there was more Shakespeare in the regional theatre than on Broadway between 1960 and 1980; what is particularly heartening is that there were more new American plays as well.) The resident theatre has produced artistically vital theatrical activity throughout America; and the acceptance of its need for—and perhaps even its right to—subsidy is evidence of a national commitment to the theatre as a link with the past and an explorer of the future, and not merely as a source of idle entertainment.

Notes

1. Margo Jones, *Theatre-in-the-Round* (New York: Rinehart, 1951), pp. 3–5.

2. Joseph Wesley Zeigler, *Regional Theatre* (Minneapolis: University of Minnesota Press, 1973), p. 17.

3. Stephen Langley, *Theatre Management in America* (New York: Drama Book Specialists, 1974), pp. 118-19.

4. Bradley G. Morison and Kay Fliehr, *In Search of an Audience* (New York: Pitman, 1968), p. 5.

5. Zeigler, p. 75.

6. John Glore, "The Empty Space and the Seattle Rep," *Theater* 10 (Summer 1979): 64.

7. André Gregory, "The Theatre of the Living Arts," *Tulane Drama Review* 11 (Summer 1967): 20.

8. Zeigler, p. 145.

9. Brooks Atkinson, *Broadway* (New York: Macmillan, 1974), p. 486.

10. *Bricks, Mortar and the Performing Arts* (New York: The Twentieth Century Fund, 1970), p. 2.

11. William J. Baumol and William G. Bowen, *Performing Arts—The Economic Dilemma* (New York: The Twentieth Century Fund, 1966), p. 41.

12. Baumol and Bowen, p. 161.

13. Richard Magat, *The Ford Foundation at Work* (New York: Plenum Press, 1979), p. 128.

14. Martin Gottfried, *A Theater Divided* (Boston: Little, Brown, 1967), p. 93.

15. Zeigler, p. 184.

16. Zeigler, p. 185.

Off Off and Other Alternatives

Joseph Cino was an overweight ex-dancer, a homosexual, an alcoholic, a drug-taker and a flamboyant Greenwich Village "character." Having given up his stage ambitions by 1958, he opened the Caffe Cino, one of many coffeehouses that sprang up in the Village in the late 1950s. The Caffe Cino quickly became a haven for other outcasts, misfits and failed or would-be performers; the long, narrow, storefront cafe had a tiny stage in the middle, where the loving host let his guests live out their fantasies by performing for each other and for any unsuspecting tourists who wandered in. Eventually some of the Cino regulars put on a play, and Off Off-Broadway was born.

That at least is the myth, and as myths go it's a pretty good one, with a happy blend of truth and almost-truth. The truth lies in the basic facts—there was a Joe Cino, and he did give his stage to anyone who wanted to use it, with a determined disregard for questions of talent or commercial appeal. Plays were produced at the Cino for almost ten years and there were even a couple of financial successes, most notably the parody musical *Dames at Sea* (1966). The mythic elements include the larger-than-life Cino himself and the collection of fellow

Joe Cino. (Photo by James D. Gossage; courtesy of the Billy Rose Theatre Collection, The New York Public Library at Lincoln Center. Astor, Lenox and Tilden Foundations)

misfits who formed around him, particularly as filtered through memory in the years since Joe Cino's suicide in 1967. (A fictionalized but highly evocative picture of the Caffe Cino's rise and fall appears in the play *Kennedy's Children* by Cino alumnus Robert Patrick.) The myth also comes in trying to pinpoint the birth of Off Off-Broadway.

The first use of that term is generally attributed to *Village Voice* critic Jerry Talmer, who was trying to call attention to a wide range of theatrical activity in New York City in 1960, theatres and productions with little in common beyond obscurity, poverty and inexperience. Actually, the roots of Off Off-Broadway are indistinguishable from the roots of Off-Broadway; for every Circle in the Square that rose from nowhere to fame and something approaching financial stability in the

1950s, hundreds of other companies died at birth or struggled on unnoticed by most of the world—the Living Theatre, for example, was quintessential Off Off-Broadway for its first ten years. But it wasn't until the early 1960s, when Off-Broadway as an institution had achieved some stability and its budgets, production values and commercial ambitions had risen significantly above the shoestring level, that it became necessary to point out that theatre of a different sort was still going on in lofts, coffeehouses and vacant stores all around Manhattan.

Even the staunchest defenders of Off Off-Broadway—for example, Michael Smith, editor of several collections of its plays—admit that "much of the new work was tentative, lacking in craft, technically crude."[1] Inexperience and shoestring budgets do not magically guarantee great theatre; and actors, directors and authors willing to work for free are usually actors, directors and authors that no one will pay. From the beginning a large number of Off Off-Broadway productions were conceived of as showcases (a term that later came to have specific legal and contractual meanings), essentially self-subsidized auditions to which agents and producers were invited in the hope that they might remember and someday hire the participants. The distinction between showcases and vanity productions was not always clear, and even those performers and writers who did have legitimate aspirations and some talent were almost always lacking in experience and thus in control over their craft.

But it was this very freedom from minimum standards and commercial pressures that allowed the alternative-to-the-alternative theatre to grow and, at least briefly, to become a fertile ground for theatrical experiment. Except perhaps for the determined showcasers, the only motivation for Off Off-Broadway artists was the desire to work; in Smith's words, "satisfaction in the doing was the only satisfaction to be had. . . . With neither money nor careers at stake, caution is unnecessary, you can do anything."[2] The assumption of commercial failure was virtually built into the system, and the opportunity to fail and fail again without shame meant, at least for some, the opportunity to learn their craft and develop their powers. Pulitzer Prize-winning dramatists Lanford Wilson and Sam Shepard both had their first plays produced Off Off-Broadway, Wilson's *So Long at the Fair* at the Caffe Cino in 1963 and

Shepard's *Cowboys* at Theatre Genesis in 1964. Tom O'Horgan, one of the most colorful and influential Broadway and Off-Broadway directors of the late 1960s, began at La Mama; Robert DeNiro, Judd Hirsch, Nick Nolte, Al Pacino and Bernadette Peters acted Off Off-Broadway; and through the 1960s and especially the 1970s dozens of plays first seen Off Off-Broadway went on to commercial productions Off-Broadway, on Broadway and in regional theatres.

Despite its enormous output (a new play every week or two for almost ten years), the Caffe Cino did not produce many plays or artists of particular merit. Lanford Wilson's *The Madness of Lady Bright*, Sam Shepard's *Icarus's Mother* and Tom Eyen's *The White Whore and the Bit Player* stand out, and director Marshall W. Mason served part of his apprenticeship at the Cino. Generally, though, Joe Cino's determined lack of objective standards—he put on what he liked or what his friends wanted to do, and his tastes and his associates ran to the outlandish and extravagant—made the Caffe Cino one of the more self-indulgently amateurish of Off Off-Broadway venues. Its importance, even at the time, was largely symbolic: it was *there*, and its continued operation in spite of zoning laws, financial pressures and creative failures seemed to prove that some unquenchable artistic force was present and had chosen Off Off-Broadway as its home. The Cino proved that a theatre of experiment, of violated rules and of personal vision could still exist after Off-Broadway had become commercialized; and even its coterie quality allowed for positive interpretation, suggesting that drama and theatre could be a vehicle for communal unity and expression.

The connection between alternative theatre and the counter-culture movements of the 1960s is a complicated one. Certainly, not all of the shoestring theatre groups in New York and around the country were politically radical or even particularly politically aware. Still, the alternative theatre was for the most part a young theatre and inevitably reflected to some degree the concerns and awareness of a younger generation of artists and audiences. Whether this manifested itself in anti-war plays, communally organized companies, attempts to reach new audiences, or coterie productions that rejected new audiences, there was an extraartistic quality to the movement, an overt or implicit belief that theatre could play a social role.

In this light it is not surprising that several early Off Off-

Broadway theatres were established by churches as a service to their congregations and communities. Ralph Cook, director of St. Mark's Theatre Genesis, spoke of "a truly indigenous theatre [in which] the actors, directors, and writers are members of a geographical community and are presenting plays . . . as an integral everyday part of the life of the community . . . and the artist is assuming his original role of tribal actor and artificer."[3] St. Mark's-in-the-Bouwerie served the neighborhood formerly known as the Lower East Side but beginning to be labeled the East Village as it becomes the center of New York's hippie community in the mid-1960s. Theatre Genesis was established in 1964 with a mission as much social as artistic; later in the decade it received some of its funding from the federal Office of Juvenile Delinquency for involving neighborhood kids in its activities. Still, Cook ran it as a playwrights' workshop, utilizing private and public readings, improvisations and full productions to guide playwrights "who are at that point where they need a continuing relationship with a stage and actors in order to evolve."[4] Theatre Genesis gave Sam Shepard his first productions, and also staged plays by Tom Sankey, Murray Mednick and Leonard Melfi.

The Judson Memorial Church in Greenwich Village began its involvement with theatre even earlier by offering a room to a member of the congregation who wanted to give a poetry reading. The church formed the Judson Poets' Theatre in 1961 to serve both the community and itself; the Reverend Al Carmines (b. 1936), assistant minister and head of the church's arts program, explained, "One need in our community was a space where new playwrights could be produced. . . . Another concern was [that] the church . . . might be exposed to the work of these playwrights and thus hear the secular prophets in our city."[5] Although Judson introduced a number of artists, its biggest discovery turned out to be Carmines himself, a talented composer and lyricist who virtually created a genre of Off Off-Broadway chamber musicals, ranging from Christmas cantatas to literary adaptations (he has a particular affinity for the works of Gertrude Stein). Other churches in New York, from Riverside Church on the edge of Harlem to St. Clements on the edge of the Broadway theatre district, also saw Off Off-Broadway theatre as a way of serving their communities.

Of course, not all Off Off-Broadway entrepreneurs were

99

social workers. Probably the most artistically significant and successful Off Off-Broadway venue of the 1960s came into being and survived because its founder worshipped playwrights, loved live performance and found her life's work in bringing the two together. If Joseph Papp of the New York Shakespeare Festival is the modern American theatre's most extraordinary producer–director–fundraiser–talentspotter–hustler–workoholic, then Ellen Stewart of La Mama must run a very close second. A fashion designer by profession, Stewart became an Off Off-Broadway producer in 1961 because she knew someone who had written a play he couldn't get staged. She founded the Café La Mama in frank imitation of the Cino, and operated it in a variety of locations and manifestations: when city officials closed down the cafe for one violation or another it moved and then moved again and then became a private club (the La Mama Experimental Theatre Club, open only to members; its flyers and advertisements did not give its address, since those who could get in already knew where it was), and finally a theatre.

Totally committed to her playwrights, Stewart subsidized La Mama with her fashion earnings until the foundation and government subsidies began to come in in the late 1960s. She fought or found her way around any obstacles—commercial producers when they mistreated her alumni, the actors' union when it tried to keep its members from working for her without pay, even the Immigration Service when it caused trouble for foreign companies she invited to play at La Mama. When publishers refused La Mama plays in the early 1960s because the authors were unknown and newspaper critics refused to come to La Mama and write the reviews that would make the authors known, Stewart accepted invitations from drama festivals in France and Denmark and sent a company to Europe in 1965 at her own expense. She got her reviews there, which led to her being taken more seriously at home, and also impressed the foreign alternative theatre community so much that there were soon satellite La Mama companies in Paris, Munich, Tel Aviv, Melbourne, Manila, Buenos Aires and Tokyo. Stewart also lent the La Mama stage and prestige to other companies, notably the Open Theatre, that needed playing space. La Mama playwrights of the 1960s included Tom Eyen, Israel Horovitz, Leonard Melfi, Megan Terry and the ubiquitous Sam Shepard. Lanford Wilson's *Balm in Gilead*, generally recog-

Ellen Stewart. (Photo by Michael Cormier)

nized as Off Off-Broadway's first original full-length play—the combination of beginning writers and low budgets usually produced one-act plays—was directed at La Mama in 1965 by Marshall W. Mason, with whom Wilson would later work so successfully in the Circle Repertory Company. La Mama's most impressive and notorious director was Tom O'Horgan, whose explorations of ritual, mime, choric speaking and, when his graduation to Off-Broadway and Broadway brought him larger budgets, elaborate staging effects had wide influence in the late 1960s.

A list of Off Off-Broadway companies could take up an entire volume, but a sampling of the longer-lasting groups will give some sense of the variety available to New York City theatregoers in the 1960s. Joseph Chaikin, a former member of the Living Theatre, formed the Open Theatre in 1964 to explore the possibilities of collaborative creation and the evocation of dream and myth in performance; and similar experimentation was done by the Performance Group, led by Richard Schechner, also editor of *The Drama Review*, which functioned for a while as a kind of house organ of the experi-

101

mental theatre movement, and by André Gregory's Manhattan Project. The Bread and Puppet Theatre used masks and larger-than-lifesize heads and bodies of the sort sometimes seen in parades in their plays of political and social criticism, often performed in the streets.The Circle Stage Company, later the CSC Repertory Company, experimented with new stagings of classical dramas, sometimes with more ambition than success. The Barr-Wilder-Albee Playwrights Unit was essentially an Off Off-Broadway operation. The American Theatre for Poets did poetic drama; the Joseph Jefferson Theatre Company revived American classics; the Octagon Theatre produced musicals; the AMAS Repertory Theatre did new black plays; the Ridiculous Theatrical Company offered wildly campy comic extravaganzas; and dozens of less specialized theatres provided a constant flow of new plays.

Off Off-Broadway was a New York City phenomenon, the product of a concentration of unemployed actors and a theatrically sophisticated and adventurous audience. But theatrical sophistication was coming to other parts of the country in the 1960s, and a by-product of the growth of regional theatre was a satellite system of smaller, sometimes just barely professional companies. In a sense, a measure of a regional theatre's success was the speed with which it became the Establishment and inspired the appearance of self-styled alternatives: before the end of the decade Washington, Los Angeles, San Francisco, Minneapolis and other resident theatre centers had small Off- and Off Off-Broadways of their own; and Boston, Chicago, Denver and other cities developed alternative theatres even in the absence of a resident Establishment.

"Alternative" did not always mean "antagonistic," as it generally did in New York, where the Off Off-Broadway community prided itself on the distance between it and the commercial theatre. Many smaller regional theatres were born as friendly supplements to the local mainstream. For example, the Washington Theater Club, which grew from an amateur community theatre to a professional company in the early 1960s, credited the larger Arena Stage for much of its success; as Artistic Director Davey Marlin-Jones explained in 1970, "Arena Stage . . . created an appetite for the theatre [but] there are things they can do better than anybody and things that are prohibitive because of their size. That automatically opened up opportunities for us."[6] The opening was for new plays, uncommercial European plays and what Marlin-Jones called "the theatre of the second chance," plays that had failed in New York but could be rediscovered in modest but imaginative productions. In short, the Washington Theater Club filled exactly the same role that the Circle in the Square and other Off-Broadway companies had filled in New York; it even advertised for a time as "Washington's professional Off-Broadway theater." It was joined in the 1970s by the Folger Theatre Group, a sort of mini-Royal Shakespeare Company formed by the Folger Shakespeare Library to alternate Shakespeare with new plays, the New Playwrights' Theatre of Washington, and the DC Black Repertory Theater.

In Boston the Charles Playhouse opened in 1957 and slowly built to modest success as a conservative resident company, and the Theater Company of Boston followed as an Off-Broadway–type alternative, offering the first American productions of such plays as Jellicoe's *The Knack* and Arden's *Live Like Pigs* along with new American plays, with casts that included at various times Stockard Channing, Blythe Danner, Robert Duvall, Dustin Hoffman, Al Pacino and Jon Voigt. Through the 1960s Boston also saw the People's Theatre, the Caravan Theatre, the Hub Theatre Centre, the Players Theatre of Boston and a half-dozen others; and as some of these died off in the 1970s they were replaced by Theatre Workshop Boston, the Reality Theatre, Boston Arts Group, Cambridge Ensemble, Boston Shakespeare Company and others, providing a fairly consistant mix of conventional and experimental theatre.

In Minneapolis the Firehouse Theater was formed in 1963, the same year the Guthrie Theater opened, as an Off-Broadway alternative, but soon found this role inadequate. As director Marlow Hotchkiss recalled,

Our goal . . . was hardly more specific than a desire to be relevant, . . . which practically meant that we staged last year's better Off-Broadway offerings. . . . But to try to do the Off-Broadway thing with unskilled actors was simply to wed the worst of both worlds. In two years the Firehouse Theater moved from a vague promise of relevance to spiritual bankrupcy. Ironically, the solution to this problem was found in yet another New York model, Off Off-Broadway.[7]

103

The Firehouse experimented with a variety of avant-garde styles and techniques and gradually developed its own focus: scripted and group-created works that purposely incorporated elements of chance and audience involvement to make the actual moment onstage part of the fictional story.

The Firehouse Theater moved to San Francisco in 1969 and found not only the resident American Conservatory Theatre but such alternative companies as the San Francisco Mime Troupe, a political street theatre that used spoken plays as well as mimes; the Julian Theatre, which began as a classical repertory company but gradually changed its focus to new plays by West Coast writers; and the Magic Theatre, also devoted to new plays (Sam Shepard's Pulitzer Prize play *Buried Child* was developed with the Magic Theatre while he was a writer in residence there, and premiered in 1978).

Chicago was a little later in developing an alternative movement, perhaps because it didn't have an establishment theatre until the Goodman Theatre formed a professional company in 1969. Within a few years, however, Chicago had a sizeable "Off-Loop" theatrical community. The Organic Theater Company developed out of a student group in 1969 and earned a reputation for inventiveness and professionalism with such productions as *Warp*, a three-part Flash Gordon–style science fiction epic, and the premiere of David Mamet's *Sexual Perversity in Chicago*. Mamet himself was cofounder of the Evanston Theatre Company, later the North Light Repertory Company. The Body Politic, Performance Community, Victory Gardens, Wisdom Bridge—by 1978 there were fifty theatre companies in the Chicago Alliance for the Performing Arts, ranging from such well-established (though always financially fragile) groups as those just named, all committed to new and experimental works, to more marginal and barely professional companies offering typical community theatre fare. (The Alliance, a mutual support organization, disbanded in 1980, partially as a result of the size and disparate goals of its membership.)

The list is potentially endless. By the late 1970s Los Angeles had about one hundred Off Off-Broadway–type theatres, many of them primarily showcases for unemployed actors, but including the experimental Odyssey Theatre Ensemble and La Mama Hollywood, the multilingual Los Angeles Actors' Theatre, the oriental-American East-West Players, and others from Actors Alley through Words and Music. The Association of

Philadelphia Theatres had eleven members in 1975; and there were experimental or new-play-producing theatres in Buffalo (American Contemporary Theatre), Omaha (Omaha Magic Theatre), Milwaukee (Theatre X), Iowa City (Iowa Theatre Lab), Seattle (Empty Space Theatre), Denver (Changing Scene) and dozens of other cities.

In Waterford, Connecticut, the Eugene O'Neill Theater Center was the site of the first National Playwrights Conference in 1965, a meeting whose success led to the establishment of an annual summer workshop where plays in progress could receive readings and full stagings in a setting deliberately off the beaten path and thus free from the pressures of critics and audiences. Critics and audiences began to take notice when the works in progress turned out to be such plays as John Guare's *House of Blue Leaves* (1966), Israel Horovitz's *The Indian Wants the Bronx* (1966) and Lanford Wilson's *Lemon Sky* (1968), all of which, along with many later O'Neill Center plays, went on to New York and regional theatre runs. The O'Neill Center continued to serve as a nursery for writing talent while expanding its operations to include complementary workshops for young directors, choreographers and critics, and also serving as the home base of the National Theatre of the Deaf, a professional touring company offering spoken and signed productions of classics and new plays.

In addition to the purely artistic alternative theatres, the political and social ferment of the 1960s produced a number of companies exploring the use of theatre as a tool for social education and persuasion. The Free Southern Theater, an integrated (later, all-black) company founded in 1964, toured small Southern towns bringing such plays as *In White America* and *Waiting for Godot* to rural black audiences, in the faith that they would understand the plays in spite of (or perhaps because of) their cultural deprivations and be inspired by the opportunity to share their responses with the black performers. El Teatro Campesino grew out of the Mexican-American farm workers' strikes of the mid-1960s as a traveling improvisational company devoted to boosting the strikers' morale, and later expanded its mission to include dramatizing the Chicano experience for Anglo audiences. In similar ways the Florida Studio Theatre, based in Sarasota, and The Playgroup Inc. of Knoxville, Tennessee, produced company-created works drawn from the experiences and history of their

105

Eugene O'Neill Theater Center: *Jesse and the Bandit Queen*, by David Freeman. Bryan Clark, Jill Eikenberry. (Photo © by Andrew B. Wile)

San Francisco Mime Troupe: *False Promises*. (Photo by Ron Blanchette)

rural audiences. The San Francisco Mime Troupe and the Bread and Puppet Theatre in New York took to the streets with plays of political satire and criticism. There were at least a dozen feminist theatre companies around the country and theatres expressing the positions or dramatizing the experiences of Marxists, pacifists, prisoners, homosexuals and the physically handicapped.

In September 1968 the Living Theatre returned to America after a four-year self-imposed exile in Europe, where Julian Beck, Judith Malina and their company had developed a wholly new style of creation and performance. In a six-month tour that began at Yale University and stopped at colleges and alternative theatres across the country, the Living Theatre offered a four-play repertoire that shocked purists and puritans, excited audiences and disturbed critics everywhere. The most conventional play they performed was a new adaptation of *Antigone* by Judith Malina that stripped away the poetry and philosophy to leave an open confrontation between a repressive state and an idealistic youth in the context of an immoral war, with obviously intentional parallels to contemporary America. The nearest to a critical success among the four was a staging of *Frankenstein* as an allegory of uncensored primal forces accidentally turned loose by a repressive society and hunted down, only to turn and destroy some of the hunters while liberating the others in a climactic orgy of love and unification. Again the topical application to the era of Woodstock, student riots and the generation gap was undisguised, although the real inventiveness of *Frankenstein* lay in the production, which featured a multi-level gridwork on which the actors stood or hung at the end of Act I to form with their bodies the outline of the giant Creature, and which was then divided into compartments representing aspects of the Creature's psyche, whose functions were dramatized in turn as the Creature came to life and self-awareness.

The third Living Theatre program, *Mysteries and Other Pieces*, was actually a collection of rehearsal exercises: an actor stood absolutely still for six minutes; a group went through a Yoga breathing exercise; another group "passed" improvised movements and sounds back and forth among themselves; members of the company scattered around the theatre died horrible deaths and were carried to a growing pile of bodies on the stage until there were none alive. The fourth piece, *Paradise Now*, combined elements of the other three: in a frequently obscure sequence of group-created "rites" (The Rite of Study, The Rite of Universal Intercourse, etc.), the company simultaneously dramatized a catalogue of contemporary social evils (e.g., "Bolivia: A Group of Revolutionaries Plot their Strategy"), a call for social action ("Hanoi/Saigon: There Is a Group Living in an Anarchist Society. What Are They Doing?"), and an outline of the process by which the soul might free itself from the shackles of society and mortality ("The Rung of Prayer," "The Rung of Love," etc.). Were that not ambitious enough, it was also the purpose of *Paradise Now* actually to produce the social and spiritual changes it dealt with, not merely to point the way. Everyone in the theatre was meant to have a mystically transforming experience; according to the Becks, "The purpose of the play is to lead to a state of being [for audience and actors] in which nonviolent revolution is possible."[8] *Paradise Now* thus required intense audience involvement, and what made it the most controversial and notorious of the Living Theatre's four productions was that it invited and demanded audience participation. What lucidity the performance had was frequently buried under the number of spectators climbing onstage to celebrate the liberation of their souls by taking off their clothes or acting out their own private dramas.

The rebirth of the Living Theatre confounded critics. While many, particularly those associated with the experimental theatre in America, were excited by the ambitiousness of the Becks' vision and the new theatrical vocabulary they had developed, most had to agree with Robert Brustein that the company "had virtually abandoned all desire to create artistic imitations";[9] that is, that they were not even trying to do what theatre traditionally did. Eric Bentley, while acknowledging that "The LT represents the most resolute attempt during the past 20 years to create a theater which would be a radical alternative to Broadway and Off Broadway," concluded that its efforts "finally evaporate in sound and fury signifying nothing," and argued that the company's simplistic politics led it to lose sight of the basic nature of theatre, substituting "exhibitionism and voyeurism" for the proper actor-audience relationship.[10]

There was also a deeper concern, best expressed by Bru-

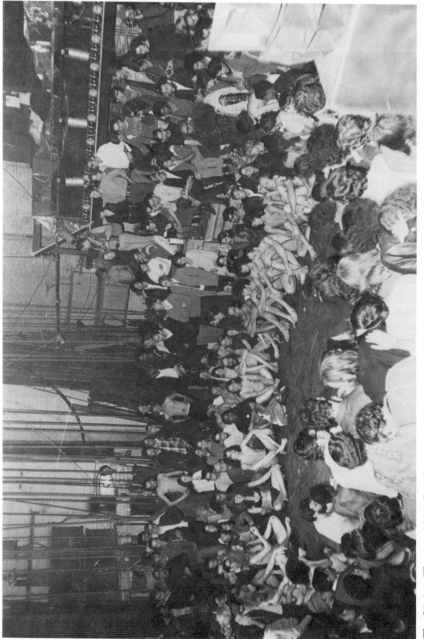

The Living Theatre 1968. *Paradise Now:* "The Vision of the Death and Resurrection of the American Indian." (Photo © 1968 by Fred W. McDarrah)

stein, who had been one of the Becks' strongest defenders four years earlier and who, as Dean of the Yale Drama School, hosted the first stop on their tour. He recognized that the company's "full-scale assault upon any separation whatever between the spectator and the stage" was a logical extension of explorations the Becks had begun ten years earlier in *The Connection*, but he was disturbed by the use to which they were putting their new mastery of this approach. Their "remarkable capacity to manipulate minds" was "extremely irresponsible" because it was directed at a predominantly young and unsophisticated audience unprepared to defend itself. Even worse, it was dishonest: while preaching anarchism, the company was tightly controlled and doctrinaire, both artistically and politically. "In spite of all the invitations to participate in free theatre . . . no spectator was ever allowed to violate the pattern of manipulated consent" or the determined order of events onstage. "It was, finally, not a vision of human freedom that one took away from *Paradise Now* but rather vague, disturbing memories of the youth rallies in Hitler's Nuremberg."[11] Walter Kerr added, "All that is being offered is a limited *illusion* of participating—and this in a theater formally dedicated to the destruction of illusion. . . . This is not participation, it is paternalism."[12]

In the year of Woodstock, campus riots and the Chicago Democratic Convention, the line between theatrical performance and real life was sometimes blurred, as was the line between anarchy and demagoguery. But the failure of the revolution to take place does not reduce the 1968 version of the Living Theatre to the status of a curious but irrelevant historical footnote. The Living Theatre tour was very significant to American theatre history; it influenced many young artists and brought into focus the work that others had been doing. There were many experimental theatre companies in America before the Living Theatre tour and more afterwards, and their styles and productions took many forms. But the Living Theatre's work, while not necessarily resembling the others closely, embodied elements common to all in a particularly visible package. In the strange, disturbing and imperfect productions of the Living Theatre, the scope and purpose of much of America's alternative theatre was crystalized. (The company itself was traumatized by the hostility its American tour raised, and split up soon afterward. The faction led by the

Becks spent the next several years in Brazil, attempting to raise the political consciousness of the peasants through street theatre. The Living Theatre regrouped in Europe in the late 1970s to develop new works.)

What the 1968–1969 Living Theatre tour made clear was that the experimental wing of Off Off-Broadway and its equivalents across the country were being shaped by four basic forces whose effects would eventually be felt in the most conservative and establishment theatres. The first of these was a de-emphasis of the text as the basis for theatrical creation. Where more conservative directors might think it their function to present an author's vision as effectively and transparently as possible or, at most, to filter the author's ideas through their own sensibility to create a collaborative product, many young directors of the 1960s began to see the text as a barely necessary evil, the raw skeleton of a theatrical work it was their job to create. Actors were encouraged to improvise on themes suggested by the text, and such improvisations might supplement or replace the written dialogue. Directors invented new business or called for new and perhaps incongruous inflections. Speeches might be reassigned, the order of scenes changed, or music or dance interpolated. As Robert Brustein complained about the work of Off Off-Broadway director Tom O'Horgan, "What has traditionally provided form and intelligence in the theatre—namely, the script—has become largely a springboard scenario for an entirely new work."[13]

Judith Malina's version of *Antigone* was essentially a stripped-down and politically simplified version of the original play, but the Performance Group's *Dionysus in 69* was a total reworking of Euripides' *The Bacchae*. Much of the original text was simply cut, and the rest was mixed with contemporary dialogue. Actors moved in and out of character, frequently commenting on the action in their own voices; and improvisation and audience involvement made every performance different. In the Open Theatre, the Firehouse Theater and some other companies the dramatist could be reduced to little more than stenographer, perhaps suggesting the basic themes of a play and then writing down and organizing the results of the actors' improvisations. Megan Terry's *Viet Rock* (1966) developed out of a series of Open Theatre discussions and improvisations based on news reports of the Vietnam

War. Terry participated in the workshops and then wrote a script based on the results. (Such collaboration had its dangers; Terry's version differed in tone from director Joseph Chaikin's sense of the work, and the resulting dispute, which Terry won, seriously weakened the company.) Jean-Claude van Itallie, "author" of the Open Theatre's *The Serpent* (1968), actually entered the creative process some months after the company had been exploring biblical themes through improvisation, and combined some of their results with new scenes of his own.

The inevitable next step was to do away with the author altogether: a director or company member might suggest a theme or subject, and the company created a theatrical expression of it. The Performance Group's *Commune* (1970) combined bits and pieces of news stories, improvisations and printed texts; the Bread and Puppet Theatre and the Pageant Players regularly created street plays out of workshops and on-the-spot improvisations. In its purest form the "play" was contentless action, like the Living Theatre's *Mysteries*, in which the actors just did things that actors do—moved or didn't move, made sounds or were silent—as ends in themselves. Some of the exercises in *Mysteries* were in fact developed by the Open Theatre and borrowed by the Becks from their former company member Joseph Chaikin. Exercises were so much a part of the Open Theatre's work that actual performance sometimes seemed like an intrusion; the company, like André Gregory's Manhattan Project, could go for long periods without feeling the need to deal with an audience.

Implicit in the deemphasis of the text was the second element that much of the American experimental theatre had in common: a mistrust of logic and rationality and of their tool, language, and an inclination to reach the audience through nonrational, nonverbal means. Dance, mime, music, ritualized movement and the direct expression of the passions became important tools for many directors and companies. Arthur Sainer, playwright and critic who worked with several radical theatre companies, later explained:

We began to understand in the 60s that the words in plays, that the physical beings in plays, that the events in plays were too often evasions, too often artifices that had to do not with truths

113

but with semblances. At best they were about *something rather than* some *thing; they were ideas describing experiences rather than the experiences.*[14]

This desire to make the theatrical moment a direct experience rather than the depiction or description of an experience led to a variety of experiments. For some companies it meant street theatre: enacting events in public spaces, frequently without warning, so that passers-by were forced to deal with the moment without knowing whether it was "real." For others it meant blending reality and fiction, or involving members of the audience directly in the action. Elements of mystic or religious ritual and ceremony were explored and incorporated into performance, in part because they represented an essentially theatrical mode that was not contaminated by literary artifice, and in part because chanting, repetition and stylized movement might affect an audience's emotions directly without being filtered through conscious thought processes.

The central event of the Performance Group's *Dionysus in 69* was the birth of the god Dionysus. The members of the company formed a tunnel with their bodies—a "birth canal" that writhed and contracted as the naked actor playing the god was pushed through it. The important point is that this was not just a clever bit of staging; for the play to work, audience and actors were supposed to experience this as an actual rebirth into godhood. Similarly, those members of the *Paradise Now* audience who responded to the "rites" of group swaying or endlessly repeated gestures by coming onstage to join in were presumably "understanding" the play better and more purely than those who stayed in their seats and tried to figure out what it meant. The Living Theatre's *Frankenstein* began with the company seated onstage meditating; the program explained that they were trying to levitate the actress in the center. If they succeeded, the performance would end; if they failed, they would go on with the play. One sensed that they actually believed that the ritual might work some night and, moreover, that if it did they would calmly leave the stage, confident that the magic moment had made the rest of the script superfluous.

The third force driving these experiments was a desire to break down the barriers—physical, rational and emotional—between actors and audiences. On the simplest level this meant finding new playing spaces. Thrust stages and theatre-in-the-round had already begun the job of breaking through the "fourth wall" of the proscenium stage. Many experimental companies carried this process further, bringing the actors out into the house or the audience onstage, or performing in spaces in which there was no clear distinction between playing and seating areas—"environmental" stagings, where the audience sat or stood more or less wherever they wanted, and the performance took place between and around them; or where the audience was forced to move around the space or among several rooms to follow the action. Attempts were made to incorporate the audience into the world of the play by violating the assumed line between reality and fiction. As early as 1959 the actors in the Living Theatre's *The Connection* stayed in character and mingled with the audience during intermission; in Tom O'Horgan's La Mama production of Paul Foster's *Tom Paine* (1967) the actors interrupted the play to discuss current events with the audience; in *Dionysus in 69* the actors repeatedly stepped out of character to speak in their own voices about their reactions to the play they were performing. The ultimate step involved incorporating the audience into the performance, either passively—actors might talk to them individually, touch them, argue with them—or actively—audience members would be allowed or invited (or required) to join in the action, as in *Paradise Now*, or to instigate it, as in the Pageant Players' *Dream Play*, in which audience members related dreams from which the players improvised actions. In 1969 the Company Theatre in Los Angeles offered *The James Joyce Memorial Liquid Theatre*, a "play" made up entirely of direct audience involvement: theatregoers were led one by one through a maze in which members of the company touched, hugged and whispered to them, and encouraged them to touch, hug and share meaningful experiences with each other. As Eric Bentley complained about the Living Theatre, such experiments in the name of what he called "the cult of intimacy" threatened to stretch the definition of theatre beyond all recognition, but the experimenters saw potential that could be defended in traditional terms:

> As the play breaks down many of the barriers between life and art, the spectator may find out something about his life through his physical entrance into art. If in Lear he learns some exalted and

*terrible truths about the human condition, in the new theatre he
may learn something of value about his personal self in a given
moment in history.*[15]

The fourth common element of the alternative theatre
movement was self-conscious theatricality, a willingness to
break down the illusion of a created reality in the play and to
exploit the possibilities of admitting openly that this was a
performance. This impulse was closely related to the desire to
use every tool possible to affect the audience and to the attempts to reduce the distance between play and audience. If
actors admitted to being actors, perhaps by changing into
costume in full view of the audience or by using stylized
nonrepresentational costumes and props, the audience would
have to collaborate in the imaginative process and would thus
be drawn into the work. Music, dance, film, masks, splitting of
roles between two or more actors, and special effects of sound
or lighting were all attempts to reach the audience on levels
other than the conscious and rational.

The American director who explored the possibilities of
open theatricality most extensively and visibly in the 1960s
was Tom O'Horgan (b. 1926). In his several productions at La
Mama and his subsequent work Off- and on Broadway, he
turned plays into openly theatrical events that gained much of
their power through breaking with the illusion of representa-
tional acting and staging. Rochelle Owens's play *Futz* (1967) is
a satiric allegory in which a farmer's carnal love for a pig, and
his neighbors' reaction to it, comment on society's fear and
repression of open sexuality. O'Horgan provided physical expression of the text's ideas and emotions through film, mime,
music and dance, turning the villagers into a many-headed
chorus of interchangeable roles so that they functioned as
Society rather than as individuals. Grotesque exaggeration
was a favorite tool of O'Horgan's; if a speech implied anger,
the actor played in a violent rage, and repressed lust manifested itself in bumps and grinds. (This sort of thing was not to
everyone's taste. Robert Brustein, with some justice, called
O'Horgan "The Busby Berkeley of Off Off-Broadway," complaining that he buried any play he directed under a mannered
style that had "a certain ephemeral charm but [was] essentially
mindless and meaningless."[16])

O'Horgan's production of the rock musical *Hair* brought his

116

Tom O'Horgan. (Photo by James D. Gossage)

methods to Broadway in 1968. As originally presented as the New York Shakespeare Festival's first production at the Public Theater, *Hair*, for all its novelty, was actually a rather conventional musical with a plot and subplots about its hippie characters and their relationships with parents and other authority figures. The play moved from the Public to a brief Off-Broadway run and was then redirected for Broadway by O'Horgan. He threw out the entire script, creating a play that was an uninterrupted sequence of songs, and then staged the songs so imaginatively that they communicated the play's spirit and ideas by themselves. (When *Hair* was filmed in 1978 a brand new book, with only general similarities to the original, was written to tie the songs together.) Singers appeared in the aisles, popped out of trap doors, climbed the walls and hung from the proscenium arch. At one notorious moment they

117

Hair. (Photo by Martha Swope)

took off their clothes while O'Horgan mocked the prurience of those who came just for that scene by dimming the lights. The singers openly used hand microphones, making no attempt to hide their awareness that this was a performance.

In Julian Barry's *Lenny* (1971), the action switched rapidly between Lenny Bruce's night club act, events in his life and his fantasies. O'Horgan compounded the complexity by deliberately mixing stage methods: a night club routine might be acted out by supporting players rather than narrated by Bruce, while an actual event would suddenly take on fantasy proportions through an incongruity of constuming or the introduction of direct audience address, cartoonlike props or giant puppets. In the Broadway production of *Jesus Christ Superstar* (1971) O'Horgan had performers lowered from the rafters or carried aloft on rising platforms, extravagant costumes and huge symbolic props, and a stage floor that was raised hydraulically to an almost vertical wall to block Judas's escape. In a tongue-in-cheek self-quotation O'Horgan gave his singers hand microphones but thinly disguised their cords as ropes and vines, implicitly thumbing his nose at those purists who would question microphone cords in bibilical Palestine.

These four elements—deemphasis of text, exploration of nonverbal and nonrational communication, attempts to break down the barriers between play and audience, and open utilization of the technology and artifice of the theatre—did not control the work of every alternative theatre of the 1960s; many, after all, were devoted to the presentation of traditional plays. But they were present to some degree and in some proportion in the independently worked-out styles and philosophies of most of those companies and artists who saw themselves as breaking away from the mainstream, and their influence was felt by all but the most rigidly conventional theatres.

(It should be noted that there were European antecedents to much of the American experimentation, some of which were direct influences: the French director Antonin Artaud's concept of a Theatre of Cruelty in which all the theatre's weapons would be used to subvert or break down the audience's presumed resistance to new ideas; the open theatricality and epic staging of the Germans Erwin Piscator and Bertolt Brecht; Polish director Jerzy Grotowski's experiments with myth and ritual; Peter Brook's imaginative Royal Shakespeare Company production of *Marat/Sade.*)

Although the period of greatest experimentation lasted ten years at the most, from the mid-1960s to the early 1970s, when the pendulum began to move back toward traditional text-based production, the influences continue to be felt. A sizable portion of a generation of American actors spent their formative years creating nontraditional theatre, and while this unquestionably released abilities in them that they might otherwise not have developed, it also delayed or prevented their mastery of some of the more conventional skills. Richard Gilman's indictment of the Living Theatre ("Whatever else it is the Living Theatre is unbelieveably untalented in the rudimentary processes of acting—speech, characterization, the assumption of new, invented being"[17]) could be applied, perhaps with less outrage, to the radical theatre in general, because those skills were not considered necessary to the type of play being produced. It is less easy to measure the effect of the period on young American playwrights. There were plenty of alternative and mainstream theatres still devoted to the dramatization of the written word, and the number of writers corrupted or discouraged by exposure to companies that did not respect the text is probably matched or exceeded by the number who were inspired to expand their dramatic vocabulary and attempt new styles and techniques as a result of exposure to radical productions. Sam Shepard, for example, did not write for the most experimental companies, but it is likely that he would not have felt confident in exploring his own fascination with ritual and magic as dramatic tools were other theatres not conducting similar experiments.

What is certain is that the alternative theatre of the 1960s, from the new playwright workshops to the wildest experiments of the radical companies, had a liberating and expansive effect on the mainstream American theatre. Even though some of the group creations and Theatre of Cruelty productions may have been artistic dead ends, they helped expand the theatrical vocabulary; and more traditional (and perhaps more skilled) directors, designers and performers have been able to incorporate some elements of the experiments into their work. Many of the Open Theatre–Living Theatre exercises, for example, have proven useful to companies attempting to develop an ensemble unity and style. Myth, ritualized action and collaborative improvisation remain part of the creative process of such writers and directors of the 1970s as Sam Shepard and Elizabeth Swados. The Broadway musical *A Chorus Line* was created Off Off-Broadway in a series of workshops, discussions and improvisational sessions during which the personal experiences of several actual Broadway dancers were combined and developed into a script. Harold Prince, the very creative director of Broadway musicals, has built on the precedents of Tom O'Horgan's Broadway work. Directors of the 1970s might choose to operate in traditional ways and traditional styles, but that was now a matter of choice. The theatrical vocabulary—the repertoire of what was known to be possible on a stage—had been substantialy enlarged, allowing new options and new applications.

The fading away of some of the experimental fervor of the late 1960s had much to do with the general disintegration of the counterculture, and much to do with the contracting national economy of the 1970s. In New York, Off Off-Broadway in general ran out of steam in the early 1970s; while there continued to be hundreds of shoestring productions each season, the proportion of purely career-oriented showcases became larger and larger. Actors' Equity, alarmed by the sight of its members acting without pay, tried repeatedly to block or control the proliferation of Off Off-Broadway showcases, only to be resisted by the very actors it was trying to protect. Outright bans on free performances having failed, Equity formulated a code in 1970 that allowed its members to work without pay only in productions that were obviously not making anyone else rich: they had to play in tiny houses, charge no admission, and run no more than ten performances. In 1974 actors desperate for work and for the chance to be discovered forced Equity to liberalize these rules, and in 1975 and again in 1978 the union's membership voted down regulations its leadership proposed.

While never fully giving up on the pay question, Equity shifted its attention to protecting an actor's stake in a workshop that might be picked up by a commercial producer, particularly one such as *A Chorus Line,* whose original actors contributed significantly to the creative process. (The original cast of *A Chorus Line* did receive a portion of the play's profits, but Equity did not want to rely on the honor and generosity of

Marshall W. Mason. (Photo by Ken Howard)

other producers.) The proposal that a showcase cast be given either first option on the roles in a subsequent commercial production or a cash payment caused little trouble; the suggestion that they be paid for their workshop services with a percentage of all the play's future profits did, especially since the only way Equity could propose to guarantee such payment was by making it the playwright's contractual obligation. Playwrights and producers argued, with some justification, that this was an unreasonable demand—several playwrights suggested ironically that if an actor got other work as a result of appearing in their plays Off Off-Broadway, they deserved a percentage of his lifetime earnings—and threatened to boycott Off Off-Broadway, which led many actors to reject their union's attempt to protect them. The issue was still unresolved at the end of the decade, but its presence testified to the extent to which Off Off-Broadway had become a step on the ladder to potential commercial success rather than a place to reject commercial success in the name of art.

Still, several of the strongest early Off Off-Broadway companies—La Mama, the Performance Group, the Judson Poets' Theatre, the Chelsea Theater Center, among others—continued to operate in the 1970s; and in the constant stream of new companies and theatres, several maintained the commitment to new plays or new production styles that had been Off Off-Broadway's original generating force.

Foremost among these was the Circle Repertory Company, founded in 1969 by four Off Off-Broadway veterans: director Marshall W. Mason (b. 1940), playwright Lanford Wilson, and actors Rob Thirkield and Tanya Berezin. The Circle Rep was conceived from the start as a permanent company that would work together to develop an ensemble style and professionalism to serve new American playwrights. Under Mason's artistic direction the company discovered its strengths in what Mason called "lyrical naturalism," the honestly emotive presentation of realistic drama with a touch of poetry. Lanford Wilson helped set the house style through such plays as *The Hot l Baltimore* (1973), *The Mound Builders* (1975) and *Talley's Folly* (1979), and acknowledged that the opportunity to write for actors he knew and a director he trusted helped him to grow as a dramatist. Other Circle Rep successes included Mark Medoff's *When You Comin' Back, Red Ryder?* (1973) and Edward J. Moore's *The Sea Horse* (1974), both, like Wilson's work, Chekhovian mood pieces dependent upon the sustained ensemble performances that were the company's hallmark.

Other noteworthy Off Off-Broadway companies of the 1970s that stood apart from the amateurism or careerism of many of their contemporaries in their serious dedication to professional standards and to the development of new plays include the Manhattan Theatre Club, Playwrights Horizons and the Hudson Guild (actually founded in 1922, but reorganized as a new play workshop in 1977). The fact that each of these companies has a record of introducing new plays that have gone on to Broadway and regional theatre success is one measure of their productivity and high standards, and also demonstrates the degree to which the best of Off Off-Broadway was moving into the American theatrical mainstream.

123

Indeed, the boundaries between Off Off-Broadway, Off-Broadway and even Broadway began to disintegrate in the 1970s, both as a result of the fluid movement of plays and actors from one level to another and through the growing professionalism of the best of the Off Off-Broadway companies. Ultimately, except for the vanity productions and showcases at one end of the scale and the expensive musicals-for-the-tired-businessman at the other (and sometimes not even then—such purely "Broadway" musicals as *A Chorus Line, Ain't Misbehavin'* and *The Best Little Whorehouse in Texas* all began in Off Off-Broadway workshops), the distinction might be no more than a legal or contractual one. A company could move officially from Off Off-Broadway to Off-Broadway status merely by signing the appropriate contract with Actors' Equity and paying its performers better, as the Circle Repertory Company did in 1976; and a single theatre might operate simultaneously on all three levels, as the New York Shakespeare Festival did.

The Shakespeare Festival, the Circle Rep, and Off-Broadway's Circle in the Square and American Place Theatre brought another alternative force to the New York City Theatre in the 1970s, that of permanent nonprofit theatrical institutions, regional repertory companies whose region was New York. These four companies and, on a smaller scale, such others as Chelsea and La Mama stood apart from the commercial pressures and *ad hoc* producing arrangements of most of New York theatre. Like resident theatres around the country they were supported to a large degree by foundation and government grants (although the Shakespeare Festival relied more on private benefactors and on the money generated by commercial productions of its plays; it lived for five years largely on the profits from *A Chorus Line*), and with permanent organizations and staffs they were able to stretch their budgets remarkably. In 1978, for example, when a single Broadway musical could cost $1,500,000 before opening night, the Shakespeare Festival mounted more than twenty productions on a budget of $7,400,000; and the Circle Rep put on seven plays and a series of staged readings on a total budget of $520,000. (Of the four, only the Circle Rep had a resident company, although the others tended to draw on a pool of regulars; the Shakespeare Festival's unofficial company included Tom Aldridge, Raul Julia, Paul Sorvino and Jane White. The Circle in the Square, still under the direction of Theodore Mann, was able to call on its famous alumni to make guest appearances when finances were tight.)

The Circle in the Square and the American Place Theatre moved into new homes in the early 1970s as a result of New York City's attempts to protect the Broadway theatre district from being engulfed by a wave of new office buildings; developers were offered zoning variances (essentially the right to build higher than the law allowed) if they incorporated new theatres into their buildings. Four new theatres, two "Broadway" houses (the Uris and the Minskoff) and two smaller homes for the Circle and the American Place, resulted before the construction boom ended in the early 1970s. Geography and environment have some commercial significance, and having new homes in the Broadway area increased the two companies' visibility and audiences; the Circle, in particular, began to be seen as a Broadway operation.

The New York Shakespeare Festival and the Circle Repertory Company also began to operate across traditional lines. Even before taking the contractual step from Off Off-Broadway to Off-Broadway status the Circle Rep had a success (*The Hot l Baltimore*) that transferred to an Off-Broadway run—interestingly, in the Circle in the Square's downtown theatre—while the company continued its regular season, and it later had both Off Off-Broadway new play workshops and Broadway transfers. The New York Shakespeare Festival was everywhere: even after withdrawing from Lincoln Center in 1977 Joseph Papp continued the summer seasons of free Shakespeare in Central Park and year-round Off-Broadway and Off Off-Broadway productions at the Public Theater, along with jazz, film and poetry programs. In addition, the Festival "adopted" many Off Off-Broadway companies and productions, giving Public Theater space to plays that deserved longer life than their workshops allowed but that had not found commercial producers. Among many such adoptees were the Riverside Church production of Miguel Pinero's *Short Eyes*, the Manhattan Theatre Club staging of David Rudkin's *Ashes*, and whole seasons of the Manhattan Project and the New Federal Theatre. Papp also knew how to exploit the commercial theatre; the Broadway and national successes of *Hair, Two Gentlemen of Verona* and *A Chorus Line* not only underwrote whole seasons at the Public, but also supported the

125

transfer to Broadway of less commercial plays that Papp wanted to give a larger audience: David Rabe's *Sticks and Bones,* Jason Miller's *That Championship Season,* and Ntozake Shange's *For Colored Girls Who Have Considered Suicide/When the Rainbow is Enuf.*

Off Off-Broadway, and the alternative theatre in general, thus joined in the partial liberation from the marketplace that the regional theatre had begun in the 1960s. The Ford Foundation made its first alternative theatre grants in 1968 and continued to support La Mama, the Open Theatre and several other companies; and the Rockefeller Foundation and National Endowment for the Arts also provided funds. Many Off Off-Broadway companies and artists were eligible for funding from the New York State Council for the Arts, and their equivalents in some other states also benefited from state and city grants. Some of the most talented young dramatists were able to write for the noncommercial theatre and still pay the rent as a result of fellowships from Ford, Guggenheim, Rockefeller or the National Endowment. The Theatre Development Fund, which had been formed to support the Broadway theatre, moved into Off Off-Broadway with a discount voucher system in 1972 and aided in the introduction of similar programs in Boston, Chicago and Minneapolis. Across the country the major foundations began to support smaller companies as well as the more-established resident theatres, with the Rockefeller Fund and the National Endowment particularly generous to promising younger theatres. The Ford-sponsored Theatre Communications Group, which had limited its support to thirteen major resident companies, was redesigned to include smaller and experimental theatres in 1972, and by 1979 had more than 165 member companies benefiting from its casting and referral services, subscription and management assistance, and other practical and moral support.

The hundreds of Off Off-Broadway companies, combined with the dozens of established regional resident theatres and their hundreds of satellite alternative companies, meant a many-times-over multiplication of the outlets available to new playwrights. For the first time in a century a beginning or developing dramatist was at least as likely to be produced outside New York City as in; and the most prolific and successful young writers moved back and forth between New York and other cities, between established and alternative companies, and between the commercial and noncommercial theatre. Lanford Wilson, for example, began at Off Off-Broadway's Caffe Cino and La Mama and returned to the Circle Repertory Company and Off-Broadway and Broadway successes, but in between he also had plays premiered at the Studio Arena in Buffalo, the Washington Theater Club, the O'Neill Center in Connecticut and the Los Angeles Center Theatre Group. Rochelle Owens has had premieres in Minneapolis and Philadelphia as well as New York; Jean-Claude van Itallie in Atlanta, Minneapolis and Los Angeles; David Mamet in Chicago; and Sam Shepard virtually everywhere: the Theatre Company of Boston, the San Francisco Magic Theatre, the Firehouse Theater of Minneapolis and the Center Theatre Group in Los Angeles, as well as London, Edinburgh and New York.

Inevitably, with hundreds of new-play-producing theatres and probably thousands of newly produced playwrights, there has been a great deal of dross. Even among the legitimately talented young writers, many lost interest in the theatre, many had only one or two plays in them, and many never progressed beyond the "promising" stage. Perhaps a dozen of the new dramatists produced by the regional and alternative theatres in the 1960s and 1970s stand out, either for a substantial body of impressive work, for one or two successes, or as the best representatives of a particular movement or subgroup; and of these, four seem to have some claim to placement in the top rank of American dramatists.

His fellow writers almost unanimously consider Sam Shepard (b. 1943) the most talented new playwright since Edward Albee, but Shepard's uncompromisingly personal vision and challenging style have kept him from achieving as wide an audience as, say, Lanford Wilson, although he has been produced all over America (with the striking exception of Broadway). Shepard's plays range from naturalistic Pinteresque studies in the tensions just beneath the surface of ordinary behavior (*Icarus's Mother*, 1965) to complex symbolic fantasies (*Cowboy Mouth*, 1971), but two themes are central to his work: the faith that magic exists as a part of the real world and is ignored or rejected only at great peril, and the conviction that America's salvation lies in the appreciation of and reintegration with the highest values of its past. To communicate the

127

Sam Shepard. (Photo by Ron Blanchette)

first, Shepard repeatedly incorporates elements of myth, magic and the supernatural into the content and style of his plays; for the second, his recurring image is the American cowboy, particularly the cowboy of movie and myth, symbol of a set of values that Shepard sees as the core of a once and future American greatness.

In *Operation Sidewinder* (1970), for example, an Air Force computer built in the shape of a giant rattlesnake (in itself a striking image of the dangers of dehumanized technology) turns out to be the missing element needed in an Apache Indian rite that brings on the apocalypse. The red man's religion is thus shown to have a truer grasp on reality than the white man's science, and a young white couple caught in the middle find their salvation by casting off civilization and joining the Indian rites. In *Back Bog Beast Bait* (1971) a two-headed swamp monster cannot be fought by human means but only by Cajun magic, and acceptance of the magic liberates the spirits of the doubting humans.

Other Shepard plays focus on one or the other of these themes. In *Red Cross* (1966) a man plays irresponsibly with the powers of his imagination; when his fantasies start to come true, the shock literally "blows his mind"—his head begins to hemorrhage. In *Angel City* (1976), a satire of Hollywood (where Shepard has worked as screenwriter and actor), filmmakers cynically toying with the creative magic of movies are transformed into monsters. *Fourteen Hundred Thousand* (1966), *Cowboy Mouth* (1971) and *Mad Dog Blues* (1971) condemn the emptiness of contemporary life and values, and blame it on the rejection of the past. In the first, urban characters are overwhelmed by the simple job of building a bookcase for books they don't read anyway, while ridiculing a friend's dream of living simply in a mountain cabin. In *Cowboy Mouth* two musicians yearn for a rock-and-roll savior but look in the wrong places, ignoring the magical transformation of a lobsterman (literally half man, half lobster—that is, an earlier stage in evolution) into the superman. In *Mad Dog Blues* two musicians (Shepard frequently uses musicians and rock music to characterize contemporary society) search for cosmic answers and buried treasure, encountering Jesse James, Mae West, Marlene Dietrich and Paul Bunyan along the way, and finally realize that their happiness lies in forming a community with these mythic figures.

Two of Shepard's full-length plays stand out as particularly powerful achievements. *The Tooth of Crime* (1972) is a complex study in the power of public images and self-images, modern equivalents of the magic Shepard invokes elsewhere, and shows how the way one is perceived can become objective reality. Its center is a duel of words between two enemies; one attacks with a litany of symbols of his own strength, but the other retaliates and wins by imposing symbols of weakness and insecurity on his opponent. Like many of Shepard's shorter plays, *The Tooth of Crime* is demanding in the complexity of its dramatic and symbolic vocabularies: the central figures are simultaneously an established rock musician and a rising challenger, a motorcycle gang leader and a gypsy loner, an aging cowboy and a young gunslinger, and participants in an intergalactic sporting event. Shepard draws on the symbolic and evocative power of each of these imageries while

129

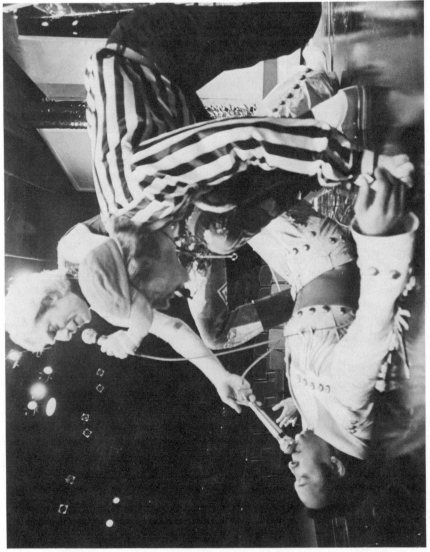

The Tooth of Crime: Ed Hall, James Eichelberger, Bruce McGill (Trinity Square Repertory Company). (Photo by William L. Smith)

leaving to his audience the job of sorting out the mixed metaphors. (In *Mad Dog Blues*, ghosts, mythic figures and movie stars function in the same reality; in *Shaved Splits* (1970), pornographic and revolutionary fantasies combine; in *The Unseen Hand* (1969), a visitor from another galaxy encounters American cowboys in a California junkyard.)

Buried Child (1978) is a work of major stature, arguably the best American play of the 1970s. In a rundown farmhouse a family of physical and spiritual cripples—an adulterous and probably incestuous mother, an alcoholic and half-senile father, and their grown sons, one with a wooden leg and one a near-moron—are visited by a relatively normal young couple, the moron's son and a girl he picked up on his journey home. At first she copes better than he does, but eventually she runs away while he feels compelled to remain, seemingly at the cost of his sanity. The inability of the present to escape the past, particularly the diseased and corrupted past, is Shepard's message, but it is not a despairing one: the grandson's return, and the parallel acceptance of past guilts symbolized by the exhumation of a baby buried in shame sometime in the past, magically revitalize the farm, whose barren soil suddenly starts producing vegetables in fantastic variety and abundance. The hope for the future lies in the unreserved acceptance of the past, says Shepard, in a play whose dramatic strength and metaphoric vision of America recall the different but equally powerful new imagery of *Who's Afraid of Virginia Woolf?* sixteen years earlier.

Lanford Wilson's (b. 1937) vision is quieter and more comfortable than Shepard's and is the basis for a body of work that tends to be quietly evocative and elegiac in tone. "We change so quickly, we in America," he said in 1980. "I guess I might be saying something like, 'Look at what you're throwing away, before you throw it away.' "[18] This quality has been present in Wilson's plays from the beginning; in *The Madness of Lady Bright* (1964), the Caffe Cino's first hit, an aging homosexual is depicted without rancor or romanticizing. He is vulger and ridiculous but also recognizably lonely and, above all, harmless, so that we can observe with charity if not with approval. But it was not until Wilson's association with the Circle Repertory Company that he could fully develop his ability to create Chekhovian worlds, in which every character has his private

131

Buried Child (The Magic Theatre, San Francisco).
(Photo by Ron Blanchette)

Lanford Wilson.
(Courtesy of the Circle Repertory Company)

drama and the strands of plot and layers of dialogue are textured musically.

The Hot l Baltimore (1973) is an almost plotless picture of life in a rundown hotel (The title suggests a neon sign with a letter burned out). The desk clerk silently loves one of the residents; a young man searches for traces of a grandfather who may or may not have lived there; a transient leaves and another remains; prostitutes entertain clients or wait for calls—virtually nothing happens except that a happy, functioning, less-than-perfect-but-far-better-than-nothing community parades before us, and we see that its destruction in the hotel's imminent demolition will represent a loss worth regretting. In *The Mound Builders* (1975), archeologists who discover an important pre-Columbian settlement in Illinois take pains to protect the site from commercial developers only to let it be destroyed through sexual jealousies, sibling rivalries and personal dis-

133

The Hot l Baltimore: Zane Lansky, Conchata Ferrell (Circle Repertory Company). (Photo by Frederick Eberstadt)

Fifth of July: Joyce Reehling, Jonathan Hogan (Circle Repertory
Company). (Photo by Ken Howard)

honesties; again the past is lost through putting false value on
the present, and again it is the smallest events of everyday life
that carry the seeds of the greatest drama.

In *Fifth of July* (1978) an embittered paraplegic Vietnam veteran returns to his family's Missouri farm with the intention of
selling it, but a day's encounters with the prospective buyers,
his widowed aunt and his loyal homosexual lover change his
mind, and he finds the beginnings of hope and a new commitment to life in keeping the farm. As with Wilson's other work,
this skeletal plot is not the entire play; each of the other
characters has his own concerns and his own discoveries, and
the play's effectiveness lies in its multileveled texture. *Talley's
Folly* (1979), part of a projected multiplay cycle about this
Missouri family, is set in 1944 and shows the wooing of the
widowed aunt from *Fifth of July* by the Jewish immigrant who

135

will become the husband she mourns in the other play. Each of them emotionally crippled by feelings of insecurity and fears of the future, they spar and stumble and waltz their way through a moonlit night to an understanding and acceptance of their need for each other, in a delicately moving romance. Much of the success of these plays comes from Wilson's connection with the Circle Repertory Company; not only has he had the luxury of writing with particular actors in mind, but the company's special strength lies in the ensemble playing and quietly evocative romanticism that his plays demand.

Two writers who would appear to rank a step below Shepard and Wilson, if only because of a smaller output, are David Mamet (b. 1947) and David Rabe (b. 1940). Chicago-based Mamet specializes in reproducing the clichés and inanities of everyday language and in showing how they meet a need for communication even as they limit it. In *The Duck Variations* (1974), two old men sit in the park exchanging misinformation and half-formed opinions on a variety of subjects, including ducks. Though virtually nothing of value is said, the simple human contact clearly plays an important part in keeping them alive with some sense of identity and dignity. *The Woods* (1977) shows a seemingly mismatched young couple spending the night in a forest; she babbles endlessly about nature and he mumbles replies. Their noncommunication almost tears them apart, but Mamet shows that it grows out of their desperate need for each other, and offers hope that partial contact is better than none. In *American Buffalo* (1977) three small-time criminals try to plan a robbery but continually get side-tracked and bogged down in trying to work out the logistics until they finally give up; again, if their lack of control over language limits them it also protects them from saying or thinking things that might break up their friendship.

The power of cliché and stereotype to cripple the spirit is the subject of Mamet's *Sexual Perversity in Chicago* (1974). The perversity is healthy heterosexuality; a couple beginning a promising romantic affair are sabotaged by their best friends, whose own sexual inadequacies—fear of men on the one hand and commitment to macho role-playing on the other—demand allies and acolytes. Unsure of their own independence, the lovers are easily drawn back into "normal" sexual mistrust and sterility by their friends' criticism. Two other Mamet plays have more theatrical effectiveness than literary depth: *A Life in*

A Life in the Theatre: Michael Nussbaum, Cosmo White (The Good-man Theatre). (Photo by Jim Clark)

the Theatre (1977) shows a fading star gradually displaced by the young actor who once idolized him; and *The Water Engine* (1976), originally a radio play, gives some texture to a conventionally melodramatic plot by retaining the radio-play-within-the-play structure on stage.

David Rabe would appear to be a prime example of a writer with one thing to say, which he says very well, but beyond which he cannot go. In three plays presented by the New York Shakespeare Festival—*The Basic Training of Pavlo Hummel* (1971), *Sticks and Bones* (1971) and *Streamers* (1976)—Rabe dramatized the damage done to the American spirit by the Vietnam war more eloquently, perhaps, than any writer in any genre. But his attempt to explore other subjects, notably in *In the Boom Boom Room* (1973), in which a go-go dancer's attempts to find some meaning to her life were offered as a metaphor for an emptiness in the national spirit, were less successful, perhaps because the subject and the metaphor held less emotional power for the dramatist.

Pavlo Hummel resembles Brecht's *Man is Man*; a harmless misfit is transformed by the military into a murderous machine, and ultimately destroyed. Pavlo's case is presented in specifically American terms; he cooperates in his own destruction by confusing his half-understood concepts of manhood and patriotism with the ethos of army discipline, and races eagerly toward his spiritual and physical death. *Sticks and Bones* focuses on how the need to deny the horrors of war corrupts our national spirit. An all-American family (inspiredly named Ozzie, Harriet, David and Ricky) is forced to acknowledge the existence of the war, because David has returned from Vietnam blinded in battle and haunted by guilt. His parents and brother cannot deal with the intrusion of his imperfection into their comfortable world; when his presence becomes unbearable they suggest that he find release from his guilt in death, and help him kill himself. As Rabe explains, "Mom and Dad are not concerned that terrible events have occurred in the world, but rather that David . . . is keeping them from being the happy family they know they must be.[19] At the end of the play they are a happy family again—America retains its sense of well-being—but only at the cost of destroying everything that the family and the nation are meant to represent.

In *Streamers* Rabe returns to a military setting, a basic training camp in which draftees await their inevitable transfers to Vietnam combat. The play's title, macabre army slang for fouled and unopened parachutes, also describes the unverbalized and perhaps even unconscious sense of inescapable doom that controls the lives of a handful of young men; and the action of the play—slightly frantic horseplay, confusions of sexual identity, class and racial tensions, and finally overt violence—although apparently unrelated to the war, is directly caused by it as the soldiers' panic mounts. If *Pavlo Hummel* dealt with the seductiveness of evil and *Sticks and Bones* with the greater evil of trying to deny evil, *Streamers* is the darkest of the three, dramatizing the horror that accompanies the discovery that absorption into the evil has become inevitable.

Streamers (Long Wharf Theatre). (Photo by Martha Swope)

A number of other writers who began Off Off-Broadway or in its equivalents, including some mentioned earlier in this chapter, have produced single plays or a body of work of some merit. Israel Horovitz (b. 1939) is best known for one powerful play, *The Indian Wants the Bronx* (1964), in which a confused Pakistani visitor to New York is terrorized by two young hoodlums in an encounter that is both a frighteningly real depiction of random street violence and a metaphor for the threat implicit in any incursion into a new culture. Similar ideas appear in other Horovitz plays—in *Line* (1967), urban tensions are dramatized in the way in which a group of people use deviousness, violence and sex to fight for the first position in a line; and in *The Primary English Class* (1975), a teacher's inability to communicate with her immigrant students triggers the fears, prejudices and capacity for violence that her liberal veneer disguised.

Terrence McNally (b. 1939) wrote a number of effective one-act antiwar plays in the late 1960s, and in the process discovered his talent for farce: in the most successful of the series, *Next* (1967), a fat, overage draftee tries desperately to fail his physical examination. McNally later wrote the entertaining if conventional Broadway farce *The Ritz* (1975), in which a straight businessman accidentally finds himself in a homosexual health club. Leonard Melfi's (b. 1935) strongest subject was the thinly concealed loneliness and insecurity that repeatedly led his characters to grasp at imperfect relationships. In his best play, *Birdbath* (1965), a young poet picks up a stupid, repressed waitress for want of anything better to do, only to be drawn to her as the depths of her fears and neuroses prove to match or even exceed his own.

Tom Eyen (b. 1941) holds the Off Off-Broadway record for once having five plays running simultaneously. Although his forte is social satire—he was a scriptwriter for the television parody soap opera *Mary Hartman, Mary Hartman*—his best play is *The White Whore and the Bit Player* (1964), a serious and haunting exploration of the mythic power of a Hollywood sex goddess. The prolific Robert Patrick (b. 1937), one of the original members of the Caffe Cino circle, has written over one hundred plays, many of the best of them understated and quietly moving studies of homosexual life; his best play is *Kennedy's Children* (1973), in which a cross-section of burned-out survivors of the 1960s express their confusion, pain and

140

loss in a fugally structured series of interlocking monologues. Among black writers, Ed Bullins (b. 1935) stands out for a series of plays including *In the Wine Time* (1968), *In New England Winter* (1971) and *Goin' a Buffalo* (1972) that dramatize the poverty, violence and inarticulate longing for something better that are part of the working-class black experience.

Two writers closely associated with the Open Theatre helped explore the possibilities of collaborative creation. Megan Terry (b. 1932) used an acting exercise called transformation (in which one of two actors improvising a scene suddenly switches to a different role or style, forcing his partner to improvise a response) as the structural basis for plays in which a small cast could fluidly fill a variety of roles (*Viet Rock*, 1966), in which the many levels of a relationship could be literalized (*Keep Tightly Closed in a Cool Dry Place*, 1965), or in which a series of separate portraits and encounters played by the same actors could blend into archetypes (*Calm Down Mother*, 1965); virtually all of her plays were created with members of the company rather than being presented to them as finished texts. Jean-Claude van Itallie's (b. 1936) three-play program *America Hurrah* (1965) also utilized the Open Theatre's improvisational skills, although the plays did not grow out of workshops as Terry's did. The best of the three, originally called *American Hurrah* but retitled *Motel* when presented with the others, attacks American philisitinism by showing motel guests vandalizing their room while the manager blindly sings the praises of its kitsch-filled decor; to stress the monstrous tastelessness of both the destruction and the thing being destroyed, the three actors are encased in grotesque papier-maché heads and bodies. In *The Serpent* (1968), van Itallie added a structure and a commenting chorus to a series of company-developed biblical improvisations to create a mythic presentation of the creation myth.

By 1980 virtually all these writers had been produced on Broadway or in major resident theatres, and Wilson or Mamet or Bullins might even be considered "establishment" writers by a younger generation. The mainstream American theatre, which had been forced to expand in the late 1950s when Off-Broadway introduced new artists and new styles, and to expand again in the late 1960s when resident theatres introduced new audiences and new organizational and financial structures, had expanded once again to recognize the talent and authority of new writers and theatrical artists with new dramatic and theatrical vocabularies.

Notes

1. Michael Smith, ed., *The Best of Off Off-Broadway* (New York: Dutton, 1969), p. 12.

2. Smith, p. 16.

3. Ralph Cook, "Theatre Genesis," in *Eight Plays from Off-Off Broadway,* ed. Nick Orzel and Michael Smith (Indianapolis: the Bobbs-Merrill Company, 1966), p. 94.

4. Cook, p. 93.

5. Al Carmines, "The Judson Poets' Theatre," in *Eight Plays,* p. 123.

6. Davey Marlin-Jones, "The Washington Theatre Club," *Players* 45 (August 1970): 290.

7. Marlow Hotchkiss, as quoted in Arthur Sainer, *The Radical Theatre Notebook* (New York: Avon Books, 1975), p. 30.

8. Julian Beck and Judith Malina, as quoted in Pierre Biner, *The Living Theatre* (New York: Avon Books, 1972), p. 174.

9. Robert Brustein, *The Third Theatre* (New York: Alfred A. Knopf, 1969), p. xv.

10. Eric Bentley, "I Reject the Living Theater," *New York Times,* 20 Oct. 1968, Sec. 2, p. 1.

11. Brustein, pp. xiv–xvii.

12. Walter Kerr, *God on the Gymnasium Floor* (New York: Dell Publishing Co., 1973), pp. 55–56.

13. Brustein, p. 70.

14. Sainer, p. 115.

15. Sainer, p. 79.

16. Brustein, pp. 69-70.

17. Richard Gilman, "It's a Show," *New Republic,* 9 Nov. 1968, p. 30.

18. Lanford Wilson, as quoted in Robert Berkvist, "Lanford Wilson—Can He Score on Broadway?" *New York Times,* 17 Feb. 1980, Sec. 2, p. 33.

19. David Rabe, *The Basic Training of Pavlo Hummel and Sticks and Bones* (New York: The Viking Press, 1973), pp. 225–26.

CHAPTER 5

Broadway

Of course no one, with the possible exception of Margo Jones, could have predicted in 1950 that the American theatre would expand and evolve as excitingly as it did in the next three decades. At midcentury, critic John Chapman could still casually start a sentence, "The New York theatre season—which means the American theatre season,"[1] and any attempts to measure the health or forecast the future of theatre in America inevitably focused on the health and prospects of the theatrical community around Times Square. And at midcentury there was every reason to think that the Broadway theatre was entering a Golden Age:

> *By the end of 1950, Broadway producers were optimistic about new playwrights on the theatrical horizon; technical innovations in production and staging, and the increased public support for better-written American drama. Critics pointed out that long-running plays in the 1940s, such as* The Glass Menagerie, Detective Story, *and* Death of a Salesman, *were far superior to the popular fare of the 1910s, and that audiences were developing a more literary appreciation for drama.*[2]

The new young dramatists of the 1940s—Williams, Miller and others—could be expected to grow as artists in the next decade, and the most popular directors—Clurman, Kazan,

Logan, Abbott—were at the peak of their powers. (In the next two decades they would be joined by Gower Champion, Mike Nichols, Harold Prince, Alan Schneider and others.) Even the Broadway producers of the next three decades were generally already on the scene: Roger L. Stevens and Robert Whitehead, who together or separately would produce *Cat on a Hot tin Roof*, *Bus Stop*, *The Price* and dozens of others (Whitehead would later be a founding director of the Repertory Theater of Lincoln Center, and Stevens Chairman of the National Council on the Arts); Alexander Cohen, whose speciality would be import-export, producing London hits *(Beyond the Fringe)* in New York and New York successes *(Plaza Suite, Applause)* in London; and Kermit Bloomgarden *(Death of a Salesman, The Diary of Anne Frank, The Music Man)*. Harold Prince was learning his trade as an assistant to George Abbott and would become one of Broadway's most active and successful producers *(Pajama Game, West Side Story, Fiddler on the Roof* and the musicals of Stephen Sondheim).

One producer deserves special mention. David Merrick, who began in 1949, was the most active, most successful and most colorful Broadway producer of the next three decades. He not only helped create some of Broadway's greatest successes—*Fanny, Look Back in Anger, Gypsy, Becket, Oliver* and *Hello, Dolly!* among others—but his seemingly unerring commercial sense and his audacious instinct for publicity earned him a place in Broadway folklore. A volume could be devoted to Merrick anecdotes—his feuds with critics, his publicity stunts—but one will do: in 1961 he found a group of ordinary citizens with the same names as the major newspaper drama critics and quoted their praise of his current show in his ads. More significantly, Merrick's business sense led him to put some of his Broadway profits into a tax-exempt foundation, which could then afford to bring to Broadway such worthy but uncommercial ventures as the plays of John Osborne and the *Marat/Sade*. In 1966 Otis L. Guernsey, Jr. called Merrick

> *an individual whose contribution to the American theater is so wide and* continuous *that he's in a class of achievement by himself. . . . Merrick has elevated and enriched the American theater with his courage, taste and healthy avarice, and in turn it has quite properly elevated and enriched him. He livens things up generally, and it's a pleasure to have him around, not only for profit but also for fun."*[3]

144

Tennessee Williams. (Courtesy of International Creative Management)

Thus all the ingredients for optimism about Broadway's future were there in 1950: writers, directors, producers, audiences, and a serious drama, musical theatre and acting style that were at the peak of their development. As it happened, the most significant theatrical growth in the next thirty years came elsewhere, but Broadway and its resident artists contributed their share to the shape and health of the American theatre in 1980.

In the fifteen years after *A Streetcar Named Desire*, Tennessee Williams wrote nine plays, none of them with quite the same dramatic power, but including at least two that belong in the first rank of his work, and three or four others whose flaws do not keep them from being generally successful. *Cat on a Hot Tin Roof* (1955) continues Williams's mission of proving that social outcasts and misfits share a common and all-too-painful humanity with those of us who function more successfully, as well as exploring what he later called "my own credo: the difficulties of romanticism in a predominantly cynical world."[4] In the play Brick Pollitt reacts to his own aging and the greed and mendacity that surround him by withdrawing into the memory of a friendship he considers the "one great good true thing" in his life, only to be forced back into reality by his vital young wife and his life-devouring father. Unlike Blanche,

145

however, Brick is not crushed by reality; while the play avoids a simplistically happy ending, it leaves him allowing himself to be lovingly guided toward acceptance of imperfection and commitment to life.

The Night of the Iguana (1961) provides an alternative answer, the possibility of dignified and even productive surrender. Its alcoholic and all-but-defrocked minister protagonist retreats to a mountaintop hotel in Mexico for a regularly scheduled nervous breakdown, but instead of that luxury he is led to the discovery that everyone around him is as frightened of life as he is. The only difference between him and them is that they have each found ways, some more healthy or heroic than others, of functioning in spite of their fears. The realization that he is no worse off than anyone else forces him to find his own way of coping, which turns out to be a course—marriage to the hotel manager and acceptance of his own limitations—that he had earlier rejected as capitulation to the corruption of the world. Both *Cat* and *Iguana* share *Streetcar's* power to evoke compassion for, and a sense of shared humanity with, spiritual and emotional cripples; and the characters of Maggie and Big Daddy in the first, and Hannah, Shannon and Maxine in the second have the same combination of vital richness and symbolic strength that Williams gave to Stanley and Blanche.

Among Williams's other plays of this period, *Summer and Smoke* (1948) celebrates life to the extent of seeing a woman's progression from sexually repressed parson's daughter to village nymphomaniac as a story of growth and salvation, although it is marred somewhat by a pat schematic structure: the spiritual Alma and hedonistic John cross at the play's center, she to go on to acceptance of her sexuality while he is inspired to reform by her purity, so that they end up as far apart as they began. (A revised version of the play, written in 1948 but first produced in 1976 as *Eccentricities of a Nightingale,* eliminates this flaw and much of the original's heavy-handed symbolism, and may deserve ranking with Williams's best.) *Sweet Bird of Youth* (1959) diffuses its strength by digressing into satire of Hollywood and of southern politics, but its center is an effective variation on the statements of *Cat* and *Iguana:* a young man aptly named Chance who has relied on good fortune and the memory of a pure romance to keep him from having to deal with reality grows enough to face bad luck and the destruction of the fantasy, and to accept responsibility for his actions.

Williams's other plays of the 1950s are slighter or less effective, but are all clearly the work of a respectworthy writer.

Even in the 1950s, however, there was evidence of limitations to Williams's talent. His greatest weakness, it quickly became apparent, was lack of control over his greatest strengths. He was unquestionably the finest poet the American theatre had produced, blessed with what Stanley Kauffmann called a "gift for dialogue that can cut to the bone, that can use cliché with humor and poignancy, and that can combine the odd floridness of lower-class characters with his own rich rhetoric, [producing] parts that actors want to play and with which they can move audiences."[5] His special sensitivity to the outcasts and misfits of society enabled him to dramatize the experience of extreme and even bizarre characters in ways that forced audiences to recognize their shared humanity with such "freaks." When Williams was in control of his talent and sensitivity, as in *Streetcar*, the result was a play of great dramatic and emotional power; when he was not, the poetry became self-conscious, the symbolism heavy-handed, and the gothic elements more distracting than evocative.

In the late 1950s Williams's popular reputation was as a writer of shocking, sensationalistic plays: *Cat* dealt with alcoholism, impotence, and the suggestion of homosexuality; *Suddenly Last Summer* (1958) with homosexuality, cannibalism and the threat of a lobotomy; *Sweet Bird of Youth* with drugs, venereal disease and castration. None of these elements was gratuitous; each played an integral part in its play's symbolic vocabulary or thematic statements. But they could be disruptive; even an admirer like Louis Kronenberger could complain of *Cat* that "his sense of theatre sensationalizes his vision of life. . . . The sense of excess alienates; in the face of so much that is disturbing, one at best is fascinated, one is never in any vital sense disturbed."[6] To the extent to which Williams's treatment of extreme characters and situations called attention to them and away from the truths they were meant to illuminate, it exposed a writer whose inventiveness sometimes outstripped his control.

Less obviously, Williams's love of symbolism and impulse to overwrite also caused him difficulty as early as *The Glass Menagerie*, where his original script called for slide projections of symbols (e.g., blue roses) and silent movie-type titles ("Ou sont les neiges") that his producers wisely omitted, and where

147

some speeches, notably Tom's opening and closing monologues, flirt dangerously with self-parody. The symbolism of
the Streetcar, the Cat and even the Iguana is generally understated and controlled, but the impulse toward excess is evident
in *Summer and Smoke,* where a medical diagram of the body and
a marble statue of Eternity have to stand too obviously for the
demands of body and soul; in *The Rose Tattoo* (1951), where a
woman named Serafina Delle Rose has a daughter named
Rosa and a dead husband named Rosario who had a rose
tattoo on his chest and rose oil in his hair; and in *Camino Real*
(1953), whose cast of characters—Don Quixote, Casanova,
Byron, Kilroy, etc.—betrays its awkwardly allegorical ambitions.

After *The Night of the Iguana* Williams's control as a writer
seemed to evaporate completely. Although a new play appeared every year or two, and although almost every one
contained at least one scene or speech with the beauty and
power of his early work, the plays were a shambles of confused symbols, awkward plotting and grotesques who remained grotesques instead of becoming more recognizably
human. Williams explained later that the 1960s had been a
period of almost continuous mental and emotional breakdown
for him, triggered by the death of his longtime companion and
lover, and exacerbated by alcohol, drugs, real or imagined
physical ailments, and repeated failures in the theatre. But
even after he pronounced himself recovered, his continued
writing seemed more a matter of habit and compulsion than of
a still vital talent, and another danger that had been implicit
from the beginning of his career became more evident. "Williams is a dramatist of lost souls," wrote Harold Clurman in
1970. "He has no doctrine, unless it be the need for compassion."[7] The compassion had always been for his tormented
characters; now it embarrassingly began to be demanded for
their tormented creator. There had always been a strong personal element in Williams's plays: *The Glass Menagerie* was
openly autobiographical, and he happily admitted that he
identified personally with Blanche, Alma, Kilroy and Brick.
But his dramatic genius had lain in the ability to translate these
extensions of himself into living characters and even archetypes. In contrast, the burned-out painter of *In the Bar of a Tokyo
Hotel* (1969), the aging homosexual of *Small Craft Warnings*
(1972), the agoraphobic brother and sister of *Out Cry* (1973)

and the Zelda Fitzgerald of *Clothes for a Summer Hotel* (1980) are too obviously expressions of his own private pain, without the artistry that would give them resonances beyond the confessional.

If it has become less and less likely that Williams will manage a phoenixlike rebirth as O'Neill did in his last plays, his own self-evaluation ("I think I'm a minor artist who has somehow managed to create two or three major works; I'm not sure which they are")[8] is almost certainly too harsh. His domination of the serious American theatre for over a decade, his influence on other writers such as Inge and Albee, and the continuing vitality of his best plays prove him to be a major artist, though perhaps one with the misfortune to have outlived his talents.

Arthur Miller's dramatic output is both smaller—only eight original plays, one adaptation and one film between 1950 and 1980—and more consistent in quality than Williams's. While none of the later plays has quite the evocative power of *Death of a Salesman*, and some were commercial failures, Miller seems to have had a surer sense of both his strengths and his limitations. Like Williams, Miller addresses central, recurring concerns—in his case the dramatic and moral crises that arise when the world's values and definitions come in conflict with an individual's, and the criticism, when appropriate, of the society or social forces that could so violate human needs as to cause such a conflict.

Social criticism is certainly the impetus for Miller's one venture into adaptation, Ibsen's *An Enemy of the People* (1950), and for his next original play, *The Crucible* (1953). Neither Ibsen's study of the one honorable man standing up against the entire community nor Miller's picture of the Salem witch trials of the eighteenth century ever mentions or offers specific parallels to the anti-Communist mania of the early 1950s, but the implications are unmistakable and were not denied by the author. Even more than the hysteria and the injustice, Miller was enraged by a system that could demand that an individual violate his own moral sense; the protagonist of *The Crucible*, John Proctor, is given the opportunity to tell a lie—even more insidiously, a lie that will harm no one—and live, or remain true to himself and die. But *The Crucible* is more than a response to a topical issue, as subsequent revivals have shown. Even without the overtones of McCarthyism, the play works as a study of the complexities of American Puritanism (Proctor

Arthur Miller. (Photo by Inge Morath/Magnum)

is so filled with guilt for other sins real and imagined that he is tempted to confess to the crime he is innocent of, and his virtue is more than a little tinged with self-righteousness) and as a variant on a theme of Eliot's *Murder in the Cathedral* and Shaw's *St. Joan*, the temptation to do the right thing for the wrong reason.

In Miller's 1955 double bill, *A Memory of Two Mondays* is an affectionate recreation of life among workers in the Depression, while *A View from the Bridge* (later expanded into a full-length play) is a more ambitious return to the *Salesman* challenge of raising the experience of an ordinary man—a dockworker driven by passions he cannot acknowledge, much less control—to tragic stature. If the play does not quite work, it is because Miller's choice of a modern equivalent to Fate isn't majestic enough; the weakest element in *Salesman* was the suggestion that Biff's problems grew out of the Freudian confusion caused by discovering Willy with another woman, and Eddie Carbone's incestuous passion for his niece in *A View* runs the risk of making him more ludicrous than tragic. Still, Eddie's sense of confusion and alienation when his private needs lead him to violate the codes of his society is haunting and evocative in the same way that Willy Loman's final madness is.

Miller was absent from the theatre for nine years after *A View from the Bridge*, a period that included his marriage to Marilyn Monroe, for whom he wrote the film *The Misfits* (1960). He returned in 1964 with two plays produced by the new Repertory Theater of Lincoln Center, *After the Fall* and *Incident at Vichy*, which shared a new subject for Miller, the challenge of accepting the potential for evil within oneself. *Incident at Vichy* is the simpler of the two because the more schematic: a group of Jews arrested in Nazi-controlled France try to comprehend the reasons for their persecution while the one Aryan accidently placed with them comes to realize the enormity of the evil being perpetrated and his own complicity, if only passive, in it. In *After the Fall* a man about to marry for the third time questions his right to such an opportunity and leads the audience through memories of past relationships all marked by betrayal on one side or the other. The autobiographical content of the play is thinly disguised, and the original production suffered from a directorial decision to have the actress playing the role based on Marilyn Monroe imitate Monroe's appear-

151

ance and mannerisms, encouraging audiences to treat the play as a dramatized gossip column. But Miller's central question— if all of us are guilty of failing and betraying each other, what right do we have to speak of love and use it to inflict ourselves on new victims—is one worthy of a serious and responsible dramatist. And Miller's answer recalls O'Neill's in *Long Day's Journey into Night:* if, after the Fall, man *is* by nature imperfect, then he cannot condemn himself for imperfection; self-forgiveness is a foundation on which love of others can be built. Just as O'Neill's play has grown in stature as critics and audiences have been able to look beyond its autobiographical level, *After the Fall* may escape the errors of its original production to be recognized as one of Miller's finest plays.

Miller's celebration of the Common Man returns to the foreground in the remainder of his plays. In *The Price* (1968) a man who has considered himself a failure is led to realize that without guidance, support or models to follow he has consistently chosen the right over the profitable, so that everything admirable in his character and everything successful in his life is his own creation. *The Creation of the World and Other Business* (1972), as the title suggests, is a comic retelling of the Creation and the Fall, though the comedy rarely rises above the level of giving Adam and Eve New York Jewish accents. Satan's rebellion, as Miller interprets it, is the demand that Man be allowed dignity and independence, and the tragedy of the Expulsion from Eden is that a whimsical God will not accept the implications of His own creation, and Man is left not really sure of how he has failed. *The American Clock* (1980) salutes the quiet heroism of the Americans who lived through the Depression, but Miller's awkward attempt to condense the experiences of an entire generation into the adventure of a single family fails on both the naturalistic and archetypal levels.

Although no Miller play is as weak as Williams's worst, Williams's critical reputation seems the more secure, since his best plays stand up to revival and reexamination more successfully than Miller's, whose topical concerns threaten to date them. Interestingly, Miller's status is somewhat higher in Europe than in America; to foreign audiences the purely American quality of his vision and his morality is more readily recognized and appreciated as a not unflattering reflection of our culture.

In the 1950s, with both Miller and Williams still at the peak of their powers, there was basis for enthusiasm about a new maturity in American drama and in the Broadway audience that supported it. Other writers of the period reinforced this belief. William Inge (1913–1973), a protégé of Williams's, offered a kind of domesticated Williams, with misfits who were merely lonely and confused rather than grotesque, and with no problem too great for love, forgiveness and compromise to cure. In *Come Back, Little Sheba* (1950) a long-married but mismatched couple face a crisis that might end their marriage, and decide after a little consideration that they need each other more than they need the ideals and emotions that were pulling them apart. In *Picnic* (1953) marriage with or without love, and love with or without marriage, are offered as not-to-be-sneered-at substitutions for loneliness. *Bus Stop* (1955) is a charming comedy in which a would-be rodeo star and a would-be singer realize that the less glamorous people they really are are perfectly suited to each other; and *The Dark at the Top of the Stairs* (1959) shows a troubled family facing a variety of emotional crises and living through them, although not necessarily triumphing over them, by means of love and an admission of mutual dependence. (Inge's plays after 1959 were all critical and commercial failures, and he turned with no greater success to filmscripts and novels. A lonely and insecure man even at the height of his success, he found the fading of his talent unbearable, and committed suicide in 1973.)

Inge's world-view is a limited one, and his faith in the curative power of love is somewhat simplistic, giving some justice to critics such as Robert Brustein, who complained that when "whoever on stage has the capacity to cause serious trouble grows harmless as soon as we learn that they too are sad, lonely and frustrated," then "Inge avoids confronting any serious moral issues."[9] But his benign dramatization of the little stories of little people appealed to audiences in the 1950s, who found something of value in his reassurance that they did not get from more challenging writers. As Tennessee Williams wrote after Inge's death, "he loved his characters, he wrote of them with a perfect ear for their homely speech, he saw them through their difficulties with the tenderness of a parent for suffering children, and they usually came out well."[10]

Robert Anderson (b. 1917) had written plays for summer

stock and community theatres for over a decade before his first Broadway play, *Tea and Sympathy* (1953), whose treatment of a boy's fear of being homosexual and whose proposed cure (seduction by a sympathetic older woman) seemed more liberated and sensitive, and less contrived, at the time than they do in retrospect. Although he wrote several more plays over the next two decades, Anderson's only other commercial success was *You Know I Can't Hear You When the Water's Running* (1967), a program of four witty but essentially trivial comic sketches. Paddy Chayefsky (1923–1981), a successful television writer, had some Broadway successes, notably *The Tenth Man* (1959), before devoting himself to screenwriting. Archibald MacLeish's *JB* (1958), a modern-dress version of the story of Job, may have impressed audiences more with the novelty of being in verse than with the merits of its ideas or dramaturgy, and Lorraine Hansberry's *A Raisin in the Sun* (1959) was one of the few plays by a black writer about black characters (here, a middle-class family moving into a white neighborhood) to achieve critical and popular success on Broadway. And of course each season had its share of light, all-but-forgettable comedies, of which F. Hugh Herbert's *The Moon is Blue* (1951), John Patrick's *The Teahouse of the August Moon* (1952) and Thornton Wilder's *The Matchmaker* (1955—the play is best known as the basis of the musical *Hello, Dolly!*) are both typical and perhaps the least easily forgotten.

The most important theatrical development of the 1950s, from the purely literary perspective, was the discovery of the posthumous plays of Eugene O'Neill and the resulting reevaluation of his entire career. As indicated in Chapter 2, the Off-Broadway production of *The Iceman Cometh* in 1956 revived critical and public interest in the almost forgotten dramatist, and led O'Neill's widow to release for production a play O'Neill had wanted to keep suppressed for twenty-five years after his death, *Long Day's Journey into Night*. The Broadway production in 1956 made it clear that this play was as far superior to anything else O'Neill wrote in his long career as his earlier plays were to other American drama of the 1920s. *Long Day's Journey* was followed by other posthumous plays, *A Touch of the Poet* (1958), *Hughie* (published 1959, Broadway 1964) and *More Stately Mansions* (1967) and by revivals of earlier O'Neill plays. They weren't all masterpieces and they weren't all successes, but they confirmed the rediscovery of O'Neill's greatness and his restoration to the highest ranking among American dramatists.

In the 1960s, with Tennessee Williams in a serious and seemingly irreversible artistic decline, Arthur Miller writing infrequently, and the other dramatists of the 1950s either unable to repeat their earlier successes or no longer active, attention and expectations turned to younger playwrights. Unfortunately, only one member of the Off-Broadway generation, Edward Albee, was able to make a successful transition to Broadway, and only *Who's Afraid of Virginia Woolf?* (1962), with its passionate and frightening new vision of America, really fulfilled the promise of his Off-Broadway plays. Much of Albee's work in the 1960s and 1970s was marked by unrealized ambitiousness—the confused allegory of *Tiny Alice* (1964) and the insufficiently evocative allegory of *The Lady from Dubuque* (1980)—or by lifelessness—the cold, mannered picture of empty relationships in *All Over* (1971). Only *A Delicate Balance* (1966), which covered some of the same thematic ground as *Virginia Woolf*, had much of its energy. Still, Albee was clearly an ambitious and dedicated writer, and he did have considerable talent, particularly with language. Most other Off-Broadway writers of the early 1960s and Off Off-Broadway writers of the late 1960s were temperamentally ill suited to Broadway, and few tried (or were invited) to make the leap, so Albee remained Broadway's resident serious dramatist.

The most important new Broadway playwright of the 1960s was not an ambitiously serious dramatist, but a former television gagwriter with a Midas touch. Neil Simon (b. 1927) is—in purely financial terms—the most successful playwright in the history of the world, with (among other records) more Broadway performances of his plays in the 1960s than Williams, Miller, Albee, Inge, Pinter, Osborne and Rodgers put together. Simon's first Broadway comedy was produced in 1961, and he averaged close to a play a year for the next two decades, which meant that there was rarely a season without two, and sometimes four, of his plays running simultaneously.

Oddly, there is nothing particularly distinctive about the premises, plots or characterizations of most of Simon's comedies. *Come Blow Your Horn* (1961) is about a shy young man trying to emulate his playboy older brother; *Last of the Red Hot Lovers* (1969) is about a shy middle-aged man trying to have his first extramarital affair; *The Sunshine Boys* (1972) is about two

155

old show business partners who have grown to hate each other; and the musical *They're Playing Our Song* (1979) is about two young show business partners who fall in love. Only *The Odd Couple* (1965) is built on an original comic insight. As Walter Kerr notes, its premise "is already a home truth: two men who don't get along with their wives will probably not get along with each other *in exactly the same way.* . . . It's a foolproof stage situation that is likely to keep the play around until it's as old as 'Charley's Aunt.' "[11]

Simon is essentially a joke writer. His plays are filled to overflowing with one-liners and two-liners, so many that the occasional dud is hardly noticed. He is also a master of comic rhythm, able to structure a string of jokes so that each one feeds on the laughter of the last. This skillful but essentially mechanical manipulation of audience response has led to the charge that Simon's talent is a limited one:

For me, Simon is the most skillful playwright to have surfaced in the sixties. Not the best. The most skillful. What keeps him from being the best is that with all his skill he is trivial: you don't even remember what Barefoot in the Park *was about when you're applauding the curtain calls. He is almost afraid to let a moment pass without laughter.*[12]

Certainly it is true that Simon's characters tend to sound alike: they wisecrack compulsively, they explode in anger or frustration at regular intervals, and they speak in the rhythms of jokes rather than of realistic dialogue.

Simon himself has been particularly sensitive to the charge that his plays are shallow and unrealistic, and has made several attempts to deepen them. *The Gingerbread Lady* (1970), his only completely serious play, was also his only real failure, and the touches of pathos or darker characterization in such plays as *Last of the Red Hot Lovers*, *The Sunshine Boys* and *Chapter Two* (1977) have generally been awkward and heavy-handed. In the mid-1970s Simon turned part of his attention to films, with uneven success, but *The Goodbye Girl* (1977) has a warmth and depth that most of the stage plays lack.

Neil Simon has been an embarrassment to the critics. It is easy to point out the flaws in his plays and to bemoan their success. Yet it is also undeniable that, whatever one thinks about the intrinsic merit of what he does, he does it better than

anyone else. As the essentially unsympathetic Stanley Kauffmann conceded in 1970, "Simon exemplifies Broadway at its
current top level of operation. If there is going to be a commercial theater—and there certainly *is* going to be one of some
kind—it might as well be adroitly practiced."[13]

As indicated in Chapter 4, the boundaries between Broadway and Off- and Off Off-Broadway, and between New York
and the regional theatre, began to disintegrate in the 1970s;
and a list of the most interesting new Broadway dramatists of
the decade would repeat names already cited: David Rabe,
Mark Medoff, David Mamet, Lanford Wilson. Also notable
were another New York Shakespeare Festival alumnus, Jason
Miller, whose *That Championship Season* (1972) showed former
high school basketball players at a twentieth reunion becoming aware of the emptiness of their lives since then; and Michael Cristofer, who explored differing reactions to the certain
knowledge of impending death in *The Shadow Box,* brought to
Broadway in 1977 after productions in Los Angeles and New
Haven.

The American musical theatre reached its zenith in the
1950s. Although the conventional, empty-headed musical
comedy "for the tired businessman" continued to be produced, as it would through the next three decades, the integrated musical drama form developed by Rodgers and Hammerstein in the 1940s became the norm and the standard of
achievement. Rodgers and Hammerstein themselves followed
South Pacific with the even more ambitious *The King and I*
(1951), in which once again they seriously considered the
cultural differences between East and West without condemn-
ing or patronizing either, and in which they depicted an emo-
tion-charged relationship between two strong individuals
without allowing it to lapse into a conventional romance. Their
next three musicals were less succesful artistically and commercially, falling victim, to some extent, to the very high
standards of their own precedents. *Me and Juliet* (1953) is best
remembered for one song, "No Other Love," for which
Rodgers had in fact lifted the music bodily from his earlier
score for the television documentary *Victory at Sea; Pipe Dream*
(1955) was an unsuccessful attempt to translate John Stein-
beck's *Sweet Thursday* into musical terms; and *Flower Drum
Song* (1958), a story of old customs and modern mores in San

157

Francisco's Chinatown, may just have been one trip too many to the well of East-West conflict for Rodgers and Hammerstein. Happily, their last collaboration was *The Sound of Music* (1959), old-fashioned, sentimental and operettalike, but filled with music and lyrics characteristic of both artists at their best, and immensely popular. (Oscar Hammerstein died in 1960, and Richard Rodgers went on to write several more musicals, alone and with various partners, until his death in 1979, but none was as innovative or successful as his work with Hart and Hammerstein.)

The highest achievement of the integrated musical came with Lerner and Loewe's *My Fair Lady* (1956). Working with a book of extraordinary strength and integrity, the adaptors were protected from any temptation they might have felt to lapse into old forms; Shaw's *Pygmalion* simply had no place for a conventional chorus line or even for a love scene between its hero and heroine. What it had were several sharply drawn characters, each of whom had to be given an appropriate and individual musical voice, and a story that trod the thin line between fairytale romance and worldly cynicism. That it could be turned into a Broadway musical at all, much less a thoroughly successful one, was evidence of how far the musical had evolved in less than twenty years.

My Fair Lady was not only a triumph of the integrated musical, but also helped to advance the genre even further. In addition to its particularly literate book, it featured an essentially unmusical hero and a nonsinging star. Rex Harrison was chosen as the ideal Henry Higgins even before the legal rights to the play were obtained. As Lerner later recalled,

> *In a very short time Higgins and Harrison became interchangeable in mind, and instead of Rex's vocal limitations becoming an inhibition, his personality and style seemed to clear away fresh creative paths. I realized that the secret in writing for him was to make certain at all times that the lyrical and musical line coincided exactly with the way one would speak the line.*[14]

The particular style of *sprechstimme* that Lerner and Loewe provided for Harrison was not only appropriate to the cool and undemonstrative Higgins, but also integrated book and music more seamlessly than ever before, as the moment at which speaking turned into singing became virtually imperceptible.

Moreover, while Harrison was not the first nonsinger in a Broadway musical—Walter Huston's "September Song" in *Knickerbocker Holiday* (1938) is almost legendary—his example opened the musical to other musically untrained performers whose acting skills enriched their plays: Robert Preston in *The Music Man* (1957), Richard Burton in *Camelot* (1960) and Glynis Johns in *A Little Night Music* (1973), among others.

My Fair Lady was followed by two other genre-stretching musicals. Frank Loesser's *The Most Happy Fella* (1965) was virtually an opera, with a minimum of spoken dialogue, an almost continuous musical line and more than thirty separate songs; it was saved from any tinge of pretentiousness by Loesser's solid footing in the popular music idiom. And Leonard Bernstein and Stephen Sondheim's *West Side Story* (1957), with book by experienced playwright Arthur Laurents, translated *Romeo and Juliet* into modern dress with little loss of tragic power and with an infusion of contemporary nervous energy that made up for the loss in poetry. By the end of the decade even an old-fashioned musical like Jule Styne and Stephen Sondheim's *Gypsy* (1959), essentially a vehicle for star Ethel Merman, had a dramatic depth and complexity that allowed Sondheim later to judge it "one of the two or three best shows ever written [and] the last good one in the Rodgers and Hammerstein form."[15]

Sondheim's comment might seem odd, since musicals "in the Rodgers and Hammerstein form" continued to be produced during the 1960s, and some, notably *Fiddler on the Roof* (1964) and *Man of La Mancha* (1965), were great popular successes. But the artistic peak that the integrated musical reached with *My Fair Lady* and *West Side Story* proved also to be an artistic dead end. There was evidently no further room for growth in the form, and as it marked time it began to stagnate. As entertaining as *Camelot, Fiddler* and *La Mancha* were, there was an old-fashioned air about them, and a sense of the mechanical; self-consciously literary plots, dramatic soliloquies and violations of convention had become as conventional as the chorus lines and strict alternations of fast and slow songs in the 1920s. In 1967 Otis L. Guernsey, Jr. noted that

> We have developed this form to the danger point of near-perfection where we can machine-make it—almost. Many of the musicals which turn up nowadays, even some of the most popular

159

*ones, are canned goods, taking some proven high-quality mate-
rial from a novel or play and processing and packaging it in
musical form.*[16]

Indeed, that same year veteran Broadway conductor Lehman
Engel published a book dissecting the integrated musical and
offering instructions and formulas for its construction.[17]

Sensing, perhaps, that another *My Fair Lady* was not likely to
appear, and faced with mounting production costs that discouraged experiment, Broadway producers turned back in the
1960s to less ambitious but seemingly still reliable formulas;
and there was little in *A Funny Thing Happened on the Way to the
Forum* (1962), *Hello, Dolly!* (1964) or *Mame* (1966), for example,
to indicate that they hadn't been written thirty or forty years
earlier. Throughout the 1960s the musical treaded water, occasionally making false starts in one direction or another, but
seemingly unable to regain its vitality or evolve into a new
form. In Guernsey's words, "the Broadway musical stage, that
traditional refuge of the tired business man, was becalmed and
rolling in mediocrity."[18]

It really wasn't until the mid-1970s that the outlines of a new
post-Rodgers-and-Hammerstein genre of Broadway musical
began to take shape, though hindsight was then able to trace
its roots back to the previous decade. Labeled variously the
Concept Musical or the Theme Musical, it was built around a
vision, as often directorial as authorial, rather than a mechanical outline or even a plot. In its most extreme form the new
musical was almost indistinguishable from a concert: *Bubbling
Brown Sugar* (1976) was an attempt to recreate the flavor of
Harlem in the 1920s through a string of musical numbers,
while *Ain't Misbehavin'* (1978) was essentially a recital of Fats
Waller songs, and *Dancin'* (1978) was a program of unrelated
dance numbers choreographed by Bob Fosse. (It is ironic that
the musical, the purest representative of the traditional and
commercial American theatre, may be the genre most affected
by the alternative theatre's experiments with deemphasizing
the text in the late 1960s.)

But even a more conventional-seeming musical could be
structured on a concept rather than a plot. As early as *West Side
Story* the generating and unifying force was not so much *Romeo
and Juliet* as the direction and choreography of Jerome Robbins;
the central image of the show was the nervous energy of

young people expressed in dance. When Tom O'Horgan threw out the plot of *Hair* and let the rock music and the physical appearance and antics of the cast carry the Broadway version, he created a musical whose medium was its message. Although *Grease* (1972) had a thin storyline, its real purpose was to recreate, through gentle and imaginative parody, the spirit of a mythic era of rock-and-roll innocence. In 1975 director-choreographer Michael Bennett turned the experiences of some Broadway dancers into a dramatic metaphor and created the decade's finest musical. *A Chorus Line* has virtually no plot—several dancers try out for a Broadway show and some are hired—but the love of dance, the excitement of theatre and the tension of the moment are what the show is about.

The history of one 1970 musical will illustrate the change from Rodgers and Hammerstein, whose innovation had been to start with a strong book and find realistic ways to integrate music into it. The origin of Stephen Sondheim's *Company* was a package of eleven one-act plays by George Furth, who intended them as a vehicle for a versatile actress. Producer-director Harold Prince saw the possibility of making a musical by using only the playlets that showed modern marriages in various states of health; to provide continuity, Prince suggested introducing a bachelor friend to visit each couple in turn. The final product used about 10 percent of Furth's original script in a musical about the bachelor's own emotional crisis, triggered by his observation of the couples around him. According to Sondheim,

> Up until Company *most musicals, if not all musicals, had plots. In fact, up until* Company, *I thought that musicals had to have very strong plots. . . . We realized early on that the kind of song that would not work in the show was the Rodgers and Hammerstein kind of song in which the characters reach a certain point and then sing their emotions. . . . All the songs had to be used . . . in a Brechtian way as comment and counterpoint. . . . The style was different from anything else that had been going on.*[19]

Company is an unchronological string of vignettes with no real story, but rather a subject—marriage—and an attitude—mixed respect and wariness—toward it.

A Chorus Line may well be the archetypal Broadway musical

161

A Chorus Line. (Photo by Martha Swope)

of the 1970s, but the team of composer-lyricist Sondheim and producer-director Prince was the most active and creative in exploring and stretching the boundaries of the new musical. Sondheim (b. 1930) had been a protégé of Oscar Hammerstein and began at the top, collaborating with Leonard Bernstein on *West Side Story*. Prince (b. 1928), one of the most successful Broadway producers of the 1950s and 1960s, began directing in the 1960s and soon found his talents for shaping and editing a text and for creating striking visual metaphors and staging effects. Through the 1970s they collaborated (with various librettists) on a series of award-winning and genre-stretching musicals: *Follies* (1971), a study in memory and fantasy in which past, present and what-if appeared onstage simultaneously; *A Little Night Music* (1973), an attempt to capture the dreamlike atmosphere and waltz tempo of operetta without using any of its conventions; *Pacific Overtures* (1976), a virtual opera depicting the nineteenth-century opening of Japan through Japanese eyes and Japanese stage conventions; and

162

Sweeney Todd (1979), a Grand Guignol opera. Somewhere in the intersection between Sondheim's ambitious visions, *A Chorus Line*'s metaphoric intensity and *Grease*'s encapsulation of a *zeitgeist*, a new future for the Broadway musical was taking shape.

It is a truth universally acknowledged, that this Broadway season (whatever year this is) is the worst ever, that fewer plays are being produced than ever before, and fewer of them are of any quality. Rising costs and union featherbedding have made the production of anything but lowest-common-denominator crowd-pleasers impossible, and rising ticket prices are scaring away what's left of the shrinking audience. The end of Broadway, and of civilization as we know it, is at hand.

Broadway Cassandras can always find evidence to support their cries of woe. There were more than 260 shows in the 1927–1928 Broadway season, and only sixty-nine in 1949–1950

163

Company: Larry Kert and cast. (Photo by Martha Swope)

and fifty-four in 1972–1973. In a given week in 1927 forty-seven shows were running; in the 1950s and 1960s the number averaged twenty-three. Adjusted for inflation, box office receipts dropped by one-third between 1930 and 1950 and remained flat for the next fifteen years.[20] In the 1950s and 1960s there were fewer than half as many theatres on Broadway as there had been in the 1920s. As veteran critic Brooks Atkinson observed about the state of Broadway in 1950,

> *If the theater were a rational industry with long-range capital and management and if it were operated primarily for profit, logic would have pronounced it a failure. After the business expansion of the first two decades, and after the artistic achieve-*

ments of the twenties, the Broadway theater had dropped to the level of the first years of the century. In similar circumstances, Studebaker and Packard automobiles went out of business.[21]

Of course statistics can lie, or at least mislead. There were indeed several seasons in the late 1920s when the number of new Broadway productions approached or exceeded 200, but they were as much an anomaly in the general pattern as the Roaring Twenties were in the cultural and economic history of the nation. Before and after that period the annual number averaged around 125, a total that included touring shows, limited runs and some productions that would now be labeled Off-Broadway. From 1940 to 1980 the annual totals floated in the sixty-to-eighty range, occasionally dropping into the fifties but usually rebounding within a year or two. And if there were fewer shows being produced, those that got on were generally stronger; the average run for a musical more than doubled between 1927 and 1960, and the average for a play increased by 50 percent.[22]

Memory also has a way of distorting comparisons. That golden 1927–1928 season did produce *Show Boat, Strange Interlude* and *Porgy,* but it also gave the world *Lovers and Enemies* (two performances), *The First Stone* (three performances) and a total of seventy-five shows that ran less than two weeks. Burns Mantle, summarizing that season for his annual volume of Best Plays, said it "will probably be remembered in New York, should occasion arise to remember it, as one that started promisingly and failed hopelessly." Mantle's sentiments would be echoed through the years by his successors John Chapman ("The year 1950–1951 on Broadway . . . is not likely to distinguish itself in theatrical histories as anything in particular."); Louis Kronenberger ("All in all, however, [1956–1957] was a depressingly bad season."); Henry Hewes ("The deterioration of the New York climate for theatrical production . . . became mercilessly apparent in a 1962–63 season generally regarded as the worst."); and Otis Guernsey ("This year [1969–1970] it all fell in on the New York theater."), suggesting that a certain amount of woe-crying was endemic to the system.[23]

Still, as a commercial enterprise the Broadway theatre was susceptible to the problems and pressures of the marketplace, and by the mid-1960s the practical and artistic effects could no longer be denied. Production costs had increased geometri-

Harold Prince and Stephen Sondheim. (Photo by Martha Swope)

cally from 1920 on, doubling every decade. In 1950 a typical play cost $60,000 to produce, and a musical $200,000. In 1960 a musical could cost close to $500,000; in 1973 *Seesaw* was advertised as "The Million Dollar Musical" and actually lost $1,250,000; and in 1980 there was talk of $2,000,000 musicals and $600,000 plays. Part of this increase was simple inflation, part a response to a real or imagined audience demand for more elaborate productions, part the result of greatly increased union demands, many of which were justified (actors' salaries had been shamefully low at the beginning of the period) but some of which led to cries of featherbedding (the musicians' union, for example, declared several theatres that usually housed musicals "contract houses" and demanded that a quota of musicians be hired and paid even if the current play was not a musical). Although ticket prices rose during the thirty-year period, they did not keep pace with expenses: top price for a musical in 1950 was about $6.00; fifteen years later it was $9.90, advancing to $12 in 1966 and $15 in 1969, with the lowest-price seat still $2.00, less than the cost of a ticket to a first-run movie. Ticket prices didn't start to leapfrog upward until the mid-1970s, with a $17.50 top in 1975, $20 in 1976, $25 in 1978 and $30 in 1980.

Rising costs meant greater worries for Broadway businessmen. Broadway had its first $50,000,000 (in gross ticket sales) season in 1964–1965, and reached new highs in each of the next three years, but that triumphal 1967–1968 season also saw ten out of its eleven new musicals (all but *Hair*) fail, with a total loss of well over $3,000,000. Worse, the next four years saw a snowballing decline in business, hitting a ten-year low in 1972–1973, the season which also counted the lowest total number of performances ever. And though the average run of a new show was longer than ever before, that was no guarantee of financial success; for every *Fiddler on the Roof* that ran more than 3000 performances and returned its investors' money sevenfold, there was a *Rothschilds* (1970) that lasted over 500 performances without recouping more than a quarter of its cost or, worse, a *Seesaw* than ran for almost a year and lost several hundred thousand dollars *more* than its original capitalization.

The blame was placed everywhere: on the costs; on the unions; on the deterioration of the Times Square area, which made some people reluctant or afraid to go there; on the generation gap, which alienated potential young audiences from their parents' tastes; on the "theatre party ladies," brokers who booked benefit performances and demanded only light, star-filled entertainments; on the critics. The relationship between the theatre and the newspaper critics, and between some specific theatre people and some specific critics, could take up an entire volume.[24] One fact was universally accepted and bemoaned: the loss of several New York newspapers to mergers and bankruptcies in the mid-1960s left the city with fewer theatre critics, one of whom had tremendous power; *whoever* reviewed Broadway for the *New York Times* could almost singlehandedly make or break a show. To its credit the *Times* was as concerned about this situation as the theatre community was, and even went so far as to deliberately undercut itself by hiring a second, highly respected critic to offer an alternative view for its Sunday editions, but the problem seemed unsolvable and remained a source of pain and anger through and beyond the next decade.

Every attempt was made to win back the shrinking Broadway audience and attract new ones. The liquor laws were amended to allow bars in theatres starting in 1964–1965, in the hope that the prospect of a drink during intermission might make some people more willing to sit through a show. In 1967 the theatres offered a special bus service between Times Square and the East Side neighborhood of many ticket buyers; in 1972 one show offered free parking; and in 1973 another paid for a free taxi ride to or from its theatre. Complaints on the part of suburban theatregoers that the traditional 8:30 curtain meant a late and expensive night led to the decision to push performance time up to 7:30 in 1971, and complaints that this left little time for dinner moved it back to 8:00 a couple of years later. Some surveys showed audience interest in Sunday performances, and by the mid-1970s about half the shows on Broadway were offering Sunday matinees in place of the usually slow Monday night performance.

The Broadway audience has always been almost exclusively white, middle class and middle aged, and no serious attempts had been made to reach other portions of the population until that segment began to shrink. In 1967 producer David Merrick revived a sagging box office for the four-year-old *Hello, Dolly!* by putting in an all-black cast led by Pearl Bailey, and the next decade saw several all-black musicals, both originals and revivals, some of which—notably *The Wiz* (1975) and *Ain't Misbehavin'*—were successes, though still to predominantly white audiences. Similarly, the success of *Hair* led to a string of rock musicals, most of which failed to lure a new young audience to Broadway; the striking exception was *Grease,* which lasted out the decade to become the longest-running show in Broadway history.

Considerably more successful were two innovations in advertising and marketing. Amazingly, no Broadway show had made significant use of television advertising until 1972, when a commercial showing excerpts from the musical *Pippin* boosted ticket sales radically and brought in people who had never been to a Broadway show before. Television very quickly became a major marketing tool for Broadway and proved equally effective (assuming that the commercial was skillfully made) for comedies, dramas and musicals. And 1973 saw the opening of the TKTS (an abbreviation, not an acronym) Booth, a cooperative venture of the Theatre Development Fund and the League of New York Theatres at which unsold tickets were offered on the day of performance at half-price. By 1980 the TKTS Booth was selling more than 1.5 million tickets a year, well over 15 percent of the Broadway total, and the Fund's studies indicated that the vast majority of its customers would not have bought full-price tickets otherwise. What's more, since the shows available through TKTS were not announced in advance, the thousands of people who lined up each day were generally motivated by a love of theatre and a willingness to see one of several possibilities—a far cry from the traditional theatregoer who sent in his mail order months in advance or paid scalper's prices to see a specific show from a specific seat on a specific night.

Still, the increased costs and bigger risks led to greater caution on the part of Broadway producers. When even a respectable run didn't necessarily mean financial success, the search was on for the elusive "sure thing." Quickly it became obvious that experience and talent in a show's creators were no guarantee of profits; in the 1962–1963 season alone, "reliables" S. N. Behrman, Irving Berlin, Lillian Hellman, William Inge, Garson Kanin, Sidney Kingsley, S. J. Perelman, Irwin Shaw and Tennessee Williams all had plays fail, and in the next two decades no one would be immune: Edward Albee, Leonard Bernstein, Alan Jay Lerner, Arthur Miller, Richard Rodgers,

169

TKTS Booth, Duffy Square. (Courtesy of the New York Convention
& Visitors Bureau)

Stephen Sondheim, even Neil Simon. Nor were big stars sufficient insurance; among those who experienced the indignity of very brief runs were Yul Brynner, Carol Channing, Sandy Dennis, Kirk Douglas, Alfred Drake, Joel Grey, Tammy Grimes, Charlton Heston, Deborah Kerr, Jack Lemmon and Al Pacino.

Increasingly wary about untried new plays and musicals, producers turned to seemingly pretested merchandise. There had always been a certain amount of traffic between the Broadway and London theatres, with one city's biggest hits likely to be produced in the other a year or two later. But in the late 1950s Broadway producers began hedging their bets even more by importing an entire London production—cast, director, sets and all. In 1961–1962 and again the next season, more than half the Broadway successes were London or Continental productions, leading to complaints that New York was becoming just a stop on the post–West End touring circuit. Later in the decade the Broadway seasons of the APA–Phoenix company indicated an audience interest in older plays and began a rash of revivals. A pastiche recreation of the 1920s musical *No, No, Nanette* in 1971 signaled a supposed nostalgia craze and led to rewritings and restagings of musicals as old as *Irene* (1919/ 1973) and as recent as *Hair* (1968/1977).

More significantly, plays from elsewhere in New York and elsewhere in the country began to appear on Broadway with increasing frequency. *Hair* and *The Great White Hope*, both Broadway successes of 1968, had similar histories: commercial producers saw them someplace else—the New York Shakespeare Festival and the Arena Stage in Washington, respectively—and bought the rights to stage them on Broadway. In 1972 the Tony-winning Best Musical, *Two Gentlemen of Verona*, and the Best Play, *Sticks and Bones*, were both New York Shakespeare Festival productions; and, indeed, all but one of the Tony-winning plays and all but one of the Pulitzer Prize-winning plays from 1969 to 1980 were first produced somewhere other than Broadway. The Cassandras could call this evidence of a loss of creative energy, proof that the Broadway theatre as it had been known was indeed finally dying. But once again the statistics refuted them: after the low season of 1972–1973, Broadway business turned around again, breaking through the $100,000,000 mark in 1977.

What was happening was that Broadway was finding a new function in the 1970s. As Guernsey commented in 1973, "It's still true that a playscript hasn't really made it until it has appeared in New York, but the road to success no longer necessarily leads through the office of the Broadway impresario."[25] Both halves of that statement were true; Broadway was still the home of the best theatre to be found in America, but it was no longer its birthplace. It had evolved instead into a showcase, a central meeting place where Broadway expertise could contribute to the proud display of the best work of theatre artists from around America.

Notes

1. John Chapman, ed., *The Best Plays of 1951–1952* (New York: Dodd, Mead, 1952), p. 3. Other volumes in this series will be identified by brief title.

2. Abe Laufe, *Anatomy of a Hit* (New York: Hawthorn Books, 1966), p. 193.

3. *Best Plays 1965–1966*, pp. 24–25.

4. Tennessee Williams, as quoted in Lewis Funke, "Williams Revival? Ask the Playwright," *New York Times*, 8 Jan. 1970, p. 45.

5. Stanley Kauffmann, *Persons of the Drama* (New York: Harper & Row, 1976), p. 166.

6. *Best Plays 1954–1955*, p. 7.

7. Harold Clurman, "Tennessee Williams: Poet and Puritan," *New York Times*, 27 Mar. 1970, Sec. 2, p. 5.

8. Tennessee Williams, as quoted in Jim Gaines, "A Talk About Life and Style with Tennessee Williams," *Saturday Review*, 29 Apr. 1972, p. 29.

9. Robert Brustein, *Seasons of Discontent* (New York: Simon & Schuster, 1967), pp. 91–92.

10. Tennessee Williams, "To William Inge: An Homage," *New York Times*, 1 July 1973, Sec. 2, p. 8.

11. Walter Kerr, "What Simon Says," *New York Times Magazine*, 22 Mar. 1970, p. 14.

12. William Goldman, *The Season* (New York: Bantam Books, 1970), p. 320.

13. Kauffman, p. 187.

14. Alan Jay Lerner, *The Street Where I Live* (New York: W. W. Norton & Co., 1978), p. 70.

15. Stephen Sondheim, as quoted in Craig Zadan, *Sondheim & Co.* (New York: Macmillan, 1974), p. 67.

16. *Best Plays 1966–1967*, p. 7.

17. Lehman Engel, *The American Musical Theater* (New York: Macmillan, 1967).

18. *Best Plays 1967–1968*, p. 3.

19. Zadan, pp. 129–40.

20. Thomas Gale Moore, *The Economics of the American Theater* (Durham: Duke University Press, 1968), pp. 147–53.

21. Brooks Atkinson, *Broadway* (New York: Macmillan, 1974), p. 428.

22. Moore, pp. 147–52.

23. *Best Plays 1927–1928*, p. 3; *1950–1951*, p. 3; *1956–1957*, p. 3; *1962–1963*, p. 3; *1969–1970*, p. 3.

24. For a start, see the relevant chapters in Goldman and in Stuart W. Little and Arthur Cantor, *The Playmakers* (New York: E. P. Dutton, 1971).

25. *Best Plays 1972–1973*, p. vii.

Epilogue:
The American Theatre
in 1980

In the first week of January 1980, there were thirty-three shows on Broadway: ten dramas, four comedies, fourteen musicals, two revues, two cabaret/concerts and a mime show—six more productions than in January 1950, with a greater proportion of musicals.

But that was not the whole picture. During that same week there were thirty-four productions running Off-Broadway and more than eighty-five Off Off-Broadway. The road companies of *They're Playing Our Song* and *The Elephant Man* were in Chicago, and the road company of *Ain't Misbehavin'* and a pre-Broadway tryout of *The Music Man* were in Los Angeles. And that was not the whole picture. Although many regional companies were still on a Christmas break, there were more plays being performed in resident professional theatres outside New York City than in all the Broadway, Off-Broadway, Off Off-Broadway, road company and tryout theatres combined.

Chicago audiences, for example, had a choice of twenty-three professional theatres, offering playwrights ranging from

Lillian Hellman to Israel Horovitz, Samuel Beckett to Sam Shepard. Los Angeles had between sixty and one hundred professional companies, depending on where you draw the boundaries of that sprawling city, with something for every taste: Shakespeare, Brecht, Williams, Mamet, Simon, *The Music Man* and dozens of new American playwrights.

In San Francisco, the ACT alone was offering Shakespeare, Lillian Hellman, Noel Coward and Sam Shepard in repertory that week, and the ACT was not alone. Audiences in New Haven had a choice of Shakespeare, John Guare, Peter Handke and two American premieres; audiences in Seattle could see Ibsen's *An Enemy of the People* or Trevor Griffith's *Comedians.* In Florida, Beckett was playing in Sarasota, Brecht in St. Petersburg and Molière in Coconut Grove. One could see an Anouilh comedy in Berkeley, *The Mousetrap* in Buffalo, a Goldoni farce in Los Gatos and an original musical in Minneapolis. There was Tennessee Williams in Tucson, Arthur Miller in Stamford, Kaufman and Hart in Washington and Eugene O'Neill in Rochester, Minnesota—indeed, almost every American dramatist mentioned in this book was being performed somewhere in America. And New Year's Eve saw the birth of the nation's newest regional resident company as the Helen G. Bonfils Theatre, a $13,000,000, three-theatre complex in Denver, opened with a first week's repertory of plays by Shakespeare, Brecht and Orson Welles.

And that was just the first week in January.

The 1979–1980 Broadway season was the biggest in history, the fifth consecutive record-breaking year not only in total dollar volume ($146,000,000), which was to a large extent the result of higher ticket prices, but in total number of tickets sold (9,620,000), indicating that inflation was not driving audiences away—though it is worth noting that 17 percent of the attendance (10 percent of the income) came through the half-price TKTS booth.

It was a strong season around the country as well. The sixty-two largest regional theatres alone accounted for 614 productions of 450 different plays, with an average of one world premiere per theatre. A measure of the diversity available is the fact that the single most-produced playwright (Shakespeare) accounted for only 5 percent of the productions; and only nine other writers (Ayckbourn, Stoppard, Chekhov,

Brecht, Williams, Coward, Albee, Mamet, Shepard) were produced in seven or more of the sixty-two theatres. Not even the National Endowment for the Arts could keep an accurate count of the smaller theatre companies around the country, although it was certain that there were more than 600 of them, with annual seasons of between three and twenty or more productions each.

Back in New York, there was another significant change from 1950. Of the thirty-three shows playing on Broadway in the first week of January, only seven had begun life there. Four were imports from London (and one of those, *Bent,* was actually an American play first staged at the Eugene O'Neill Center); two were transfers from Off-Broadway and eight from Off Off-Broadway and institutional theatres in New York City; and ten were first produced elsewhere in the country, in theatres ranging from the Arena *(Loose Ends* and *The 1940's Radio Hour)* and the Tyrone Guthrie *(Teibele and her Demon)* to the Kingston Mines Theatre in Chicago *(Grease)* and the George Street Playhouse in New Brunswick, New Jersey *(King of Schnorrers).* (The remaining two were a Swiss mime troup and a touring rock concert.)

Clearly the role of Broadway in the American theatre had changed since 1950. Not only was it no longer the sole home of professional theatre in the country, but if it was still in any sense the center of American theatre it was a center to which, rather than from which, the best drama and theatre in the country flowed. Between 1970 and 1980 only one of the Tony Award–winning plays, five of the Tony musicals and one of the Pulitzer Prize plays were original Broadway productions. When one of the most frequently produced regional theatre plays of 1980 was New York City's Pulitzer Prize winner of 1979 (Shepard's *Buried Child*), and New York's Tony winner of 1980 began life in New Mexico State University's Playwright's Lab and Los Angeles's Mark Taper Forum (Mark Medoff's *Children of a Lesser God*), then Rustom Bharucha was justified in saying that "the distinctions between 'commercial theater' and 'non-profit theater' have blurred. . . . It is now difficult to talk about the regional theater without talking about Broadway,"[1] and vice-versa. Broadway was not dead, despite the cries of thirty years of Cassandras, but it was a very different Broadway in a very different American theatre.

177

Children of a Lesser God: Phyllis Frelich, John Rubinstein (Mark Taper Forum). (Courtesy of the Mark Taper Forum)

This change in the relationship between Broadway and the rest of the country's theatres, the non–New York City theatres in particular, created identity problems and ethical questions for both sides. Broadway producers, accustomed to being the generating force behind their shows, found themselves in the position of being the buyers of other people's products. Their motivation was simple and overpowering: profits. It was cheaper to restage a play or import it intact than to start from the beginning, and a play's success in Los Angeles or Minneapolis allowed for some hope that it might have a better than average chance in New York. As Martin Gottfried saw as early as 1970,

> *The main attraction of the resident theater plays is that they are already produced. They can be seen, and the producer . . . generally gets an author who has already revised his script; a director whose work has been done; key cast members, if not all of them; and a workable set design.*[2]

Most transfers to Broadway were originally produced as part of the institutional theatre's regular season, and were successful enough to attract the attention of a Broadway producer. But some producers were not satisfied with being merely the repackagers of others' creations, and some of the regional theatre and Off Off-Broadway transfers to Broadway in the 1970s were in fact thinly disguised out-of-town tryouts—projects that began with the New York producer, with a Broadway run in mind from the start. Many of the transfers from the Center Theatre Group in Los Angeles (e.g., the several Neil Simon plays) and the Goodspeed Opera House in Connecticut *(Annie)* fell into this category; either the Broadway producer offered the script to the regional theatre with the understanding that he had the option to transfer it to Broadway and that the regional theatre would share in his profits, or he gave the theatre a grant to underwrite a production in return for the commercial rights, or some combination of the two. In 1974 Broadway theatre-owner and producer James M. Nederlander admitted with unconscious cynicism that in his view

> *The regional theatres have become the tryout ground for Broadway. In other words you get a play and you try it out with Paul*

Libin [of the Circle in the Square] or you try it out with Joe Papp and, if it's good, it moves to Broadway. . . . It's a business of opportunity. If you can book hit shows into your theatre you can make money, if you don't, you lose money.[3]

Faced with statements like that, artists and artistic directors of regional and alternative theatres couldn't help feeling twinges of guilt. A lot of them took great pride in turning their backs on the commercial theatre, and any accomodation with it subjected them to the charge of selling out. If the accusation did not come from their confused consciences, it would certainly come from such watchdog critics as Gottfried:

Who would have thought that America's resident theaters—so resolutely noncommercial, so artistically pure—who would have thought that so soon after their development they would be eagerly supplying Broadway with new, and sometimes very profitable, material?[4]

and Bharucha:

Some artistic directors have never ceased to look upon Broadway as the "legitimate" theater and the non-profit theater as some kind of prodigal child destined to return to Broadway someday.[5]

Even if the financial arrangements could be justified on the grounds that they were serving the company, artistic directors who sent a resident theatre production off to Broadway seemed to be confessing that that was the "real" American theatre and that what they were doing at home was somehow inferior. Again, Gottfried was ready to tweak their noses:

The relationship of the resident theater people with Broadway is one of love-hate. On the one hand . . . they are antagonized by commercialism. . . . On the other hand, they are bitterly envious of their Broadway counterparts. . . . For all of the noisy resentment of New York, actors across the country instinctively recognize Broadway as the major theater of America.[6]

There were reasons, justifiable reasons, for a regional or alternative company to attempt a Broadway transfer. One was the desire to serve, and perhaps even save, their own theatre. While a very few artistic directors succumbed completely to the lure of freedom from annual deficits and offered their stages to any bidder, the overwhelming majority retained a primary loyalty to their own audiences. Still, if the opportunity arose to do a play that the director wanted to do anyway *and* possibly to reap a profit from a Broadway run as well, then who was exploiting whom? The master of this approach was Joseph Papp of the New York Shakespeare Festival. From the moment that *Hair* became a Broadway hit for another producer in 1968, Papp realized that if Festival productions were going to make anyone rich, it might as well be the Festival. Papp produced his own Broadway transfers thereafter, and the commercial success of *Two Gentlemen of Verona* and particularly of *A Chorus Line* helped to underwrite the Festival's other projects; *A Chorus Line*'s income of as much as five million dollars a year (from Broadway, road and foreign productions and a film sale) completely covered the Festival's Public Theater budget for several years. (When *A Chorus Line*'s profits began to dwindle in 1980, Papp found another goldmine in a Central Park production of *The Pirates of Penzance* that transferred to Broadway for what looked like a long and profitable run; Papp announced plans to invest this income rather than spending it, to build up an annuity fund on which the Festival could live for years.) Papp remained totally confident that it was the Festival that was using Broadway, and not the other way around: "You can put a show on Broadway and [still] be an alternative to Broadway."[7]

There were other benefits for a regional theatre that conquered Broadway. As Joseph Wesley Zeigler pointed out, "approval in the tough New York marketplace could prove their worth and justify their requests for financial help and loyalty at home;"[8] and Gordon Davidson of the Mark Taper Forum admitted that even without immediate profits a critical success in New York "accrues to the theater. Maybe financially . . . Certainly there are the prestige and visibility that allow the next grant or that next group of plays."[9]

Davidson also noted another benefit of a New York production: exposure for the playwright. Rightly or wrongly, plays on Broadway get more media coverage and national notice than plays in Seattle, New Haven or even Los Angeles. Davidson told of how the success of Michael Cristofer's *The Shadow Box* at the Mark Taper Forum inspired him to recommend it to other theatres, with no success. After a Broadway run that resulted in the 1977 Tony and Pulitzer Prize, *The Shadow Box* became a

181

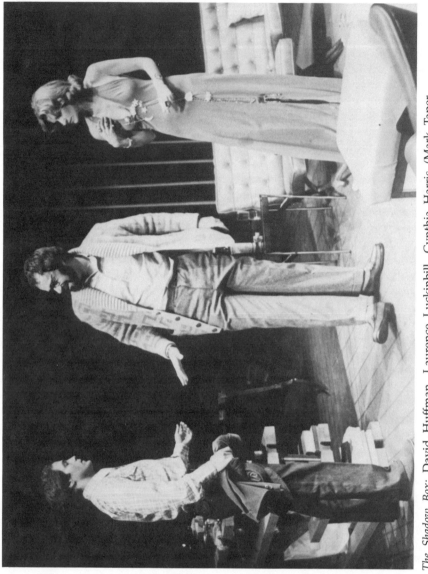

The Shadow Box: David Huffman, Laurence Luckinbill, Cynthia Harris (Mark Taper Forum). (Courtesy of the Mark Taper Forum)

staple of the regional theatre repertoire. "Once a play wins New York approval, it's easier to get it done. . . . So it is important to the playwright to have some kind of New York outing."[10] Again, Joseph Papp was particularly adept at his art; some of the profits from his Broadway successes paid for Broadway runs for such Festival plays as *That Championship Season, Sticks and Bones, For Colored Girls . . ., Miss Margarida's Way* and *Runaways*, not in any real hope of making money from the transfers, but to expose the Broadway audience to these plays and expose these plays to the publicity that would lead to other productions.

The question of Broadway's centrality remained: if, for whatever reason, regional and nonprofit theatres were motivated to risk Broadway productions, weren't they admitting that it was still the pinnacle of the American theatre? Zeigler provided a satisfactory answer. He admitted that "while the creative decline has lessened Broadway's artistic influence, it has not reduced its power. . . . Even in decline Broadway is still the only theatrical context that can assure a national position."[11] but he saw that the explanation was larger than Broadway and even than the theatre.

The power that Broadway still bore in 1980 was borrowed power; it came from being located in the intellectual, cultural, commercial and communications capital of the country:

Probably all other cities in America are nicer to live in than New York, but still it is the only ultimate American city. . . . The fulcrum of power could not be shifted—simply because New York is where the mind of the country is most concentrated. If there is to be one National Theatre . . . in America, it will have to be located . . . in the central city of New York.[12]

In short, if Broadway didn't already exist, the regional theatre would probably have had to invent it to provide a central showcase. Broadway's continuing importance was a function, not of its centrality in the American theatre, but of New York City's centrality in American society. Zeigler concluded that the question of who was to exploit whom had already been resolved:

For the first time in American history the contextual power of Broadway and the creative quality of the institutional theatre

183

> *(inside and outside New York) can combine to create a truly*
> *superior expression of the art. It is a matter not of overthrowing*
> *Broadway's power but of using it.* [13]

There remained one serious cloud on the horizon. In 1980, the year this study ends, the American people chose a new president in an election widely interpreted as a mandate to reduce government spending and reverse the direction of the government's involvement in social services, which had been growing for fifty years. Among the first cuts announced were those in the National Endowment for the Arts and the other social programs (e.g., cultural education) that had helped support the noncommercial theatre. If the new president was correct in his interpretation of the mood of the country, then it seemed certain that state and city support for the arts would soon be drastically reduced as well, while private funds might be redirected to other areas. As early as 1974 Stephen Langley had warned that "No American arts manager should be so optimistic as to believe that private and public subsidy for the arts is inevitable."[14] The possibility that there might soon be no one to make up the 40 to 60 percent deficit that seemed built into the resident theatre structure threatened to undo all the advances of the previous thirty years.

A reduction in arts funding, particularly from the public sector, *was* inevitable, and some belt-tightening was going to be necessary in the 1980s. But the essential change in the financial structure of the American theatre since 1950 seemed irreversible. Museums, symphony orchestras, opera companies, libraries and universities had gone through bad times in the past, and some had not survived, but society had never rejected the concept of their survival. The public accepted the basic principle that its cultural institutions were not meant to be self-sustaining. They deserved and would receive financial support from somewhere—from the government when rich patrons weren't available, from the foundations when the government wasn't available, from the business world when the foundations weren't available.

In many cities across America the local resident theatre companies had achieved the same sort of institutional status in the public perception since midcentury, and the likelihood that they would be told to start making a profit or die seemed remote, even in the new atmosphere of austerity. The financial challenge for the institutional theatre in America in the 1980s would not be to survive without subsidy but to find new sources of subsidy. As certain as anything could be in an uncertain world, the changes that took place in the American theatre from 1950 to 1980 were not going to be reversed.

Notes

1. Rustom Bharucha, "Anatomy of the Regional Theater," *Theater* 10 (Summer 1979): 10–13.

2. Martin Gottfried, "What Shall It Profit a Theatre If . . .?" *New York Times*, 23 August 1970, Sec. 2, p. 1.

3. James M. Nederlander, as quoted in *Producers on Producing*, ed. Stephen Langley (New York: Drama Book Specialists, 1976), pp. 301–2.

4. Gottfried, p. 1.

5. Bharucha, p. 13.

6. Martin Gottfried, *A Theater Divided* (Boston: Little, Brown, 1967), pp. 110–11.

7. Joseph Papp, as quoted in Bharucha, p. 10.

8. Joseph Wesley Zeigler, *Regional Theatre* (Minneapolis: University of Minnesota Press, 1973), p. 210.

9. Gordon Davidson, as quoted in Jules Aaron, "The Mark Taper Forum," *Theater* 10 (Summer 1979): 59.

10. Davidson, p. 58.

11. Zeigler, p. 238.

12. Zeigler, pp. 203–6.

13. Zeigler, p. 239.

14. Stephen Langley, *Theatre Management in America* (New York: Drama Book Specialists, 1974), p. 119.

185

Index

Abbott, George, 18, 20, 28, 144
ACT. *See* American Conservatory Theatre
Actor Prepares, An (Stanislavski), 15
Actors Alley, 104
Actors' Equity, 21, 26, 59–60, 77, 121–23, 124
Actor's Studio, 15–17, 88
Actors Theatre of Louisville, 89
Actor's Workshop, 61, 73, 75, 88
Adler, Stella, 15, 24
After the Fall (Miller), 73, 74, 75, 151–52
Ahmanson Theatre, 66, 70, 74, 87; *photo,* 68
Ain't Misbehavin' (Waller), 124, 160, 169, 175
Alaska Repertory Theatre, 87
Albee, Edward, 46, 65, 78, 80, 149, 177; on Broadway, 43–45, 49, 53, 169; influence, 45, 70, 102; plays analyzed, 42–45, 155; quoted on Off-Broadway, 49
Aldridge, Tom, 124
Alexander, Jane, 79
Alfred, William, 46
Alhambra Theatre, 24
Allegro (Rodgers/Hammerstein), 13
Alley Theatre, 21, 59, 83, 86, 87, 88, 89; *photo,* 85
All My Sons (Miller), 5
All Over (Albee), 155
Alternative theatre, 77, 78, 98, 103, 104–8. *See also* Experimental theatre; Off-Broadway; Off Off-Broadway
AMAS Repertory Theatre, 102
America Hurrah (van Itallie), 52, 141
American Buffalo (Mamet), 83, 136
American Clock, The (Miller), 152

American Conservatory Theatre (ACT), 65, 75, 89, 90, 104, 176; *photo,* 64
American Contemporary Theatre, 105
American Dream, The (Albee), 42–43
American Place Theatre, 46, 88, 124–25; *photo,* 47
American Playwrights Theater, 80
American Shakespeare Festival, 88
American Theatre for Poets, 102
Anderson, Maxwell, 4
Anderson, Robert, 80, 153–54
Andrew W. Mellon Foundation, 89
Angel City (Shepard), 129
Annie Get Your Gun (Berlin), 15
Another Part of the Forest (Hellman), 9
Anouilh, Jean, 65, 78, 176
Antigone (Malina), 108, 112
Antoinette Perry Award, 171, 177, 181
APA: *See* Association of Producing Artists
Applause (Strouse/Adams), 144
Arden, John, 103
Arena Stage, 21, 60, 78, 85, 102; *photo,* 84; premieres, 80, 83, 171, 177; subsidy, 87, 88, 90
Artaud, Antonin, 119
Arthur, Beatrice, 40
Ashes (Rudkin), 80, 125
Association of Philadelphia Theatres, 105
Association of Producing Artists (APA), 35, 49, 53, 63, 88, 171
As You Like It (Shakespeare), 22
Atkinson, Brooks, quoted on Broadway, 164–65; quoted on Lincoln Center, 76
Auberjonois, René, 79

Avery Fisher Hall: *photo*, 71
Ayckbourn, Alan, 70, 176

Back Bog Beast Bait (Shepard), 128–29
Bailey, Pearl, 168
Balcony, The (Genêt), 41, 46
Bald Soprano, The (Ionesco), 40, 43
Ball, William, 65, 75, 79; *photo*, 64
Balm in Gilead (Wilson), 100
Bankhead, Tallulah, 22
Barefoot in the Park (Simon), 156
Barr, Richard, 45, 70, 102
Barry, Julian, 119
Barter Theatre, 21
Basic Training of Pavlo Hummel, The (Rabe), 137, 138
Baylor College, 63
Beck, Julian, 31–35, 41–42, 108–12; *photo*, 34; quoted on Living Theatre, 33, 109
Becket (Anouilh), 144
Beckett, Samuel, 40, 46, 61, 65, 78, 176
Behrman, S. N., 73, 169
Ben-Ami, Jacob, 23
Bennett, Michael, 161
Bent (Sherman), 177
Bentley, Eric, quoted on Living Theatre, 109, 115
Berezin, Tanya, 123
Bergman, Ingrid, 70
Berlin, Irving, 11, 15, 169
Bernstein, Leonard, 159, 162, 169
Besoyan, Rick, 48
Best Little Whorehouse in Texas, The (Hall), 124
Beyond the Fringe (Bennett/Cook/Miller/Moore), 144
Bharucha, Rustom, quoted on regional theatre and Broadway, 177, 180
Bingo (Bond), 80
Birdbath (Melfi), 140
Black Crook, The (Barras), 10
Blacks, The (Genêt), 46
Blacks in the theatre: actors, 38–39, 46–48, 168–69; audiences, 24, 105, 168–69; companies, 24, 52, 89, 102, 103, 105; dramatists, 45, 51–52, 141, 154
Black Theater Workshop, 52
Blau, Herbert, 61, 73, 75
Blitzstein, Marc, 39
Bloomgarden, Kermit, 26, 144
Body Politic, 104
Bolger, Ray, 17

Bond, Edward, 80
Born Yesterday (Kanin), 9, 22
Boston Arts Group, 103
Boston Shakespeare Company, 103
Box-Mao-Box (Albee), 80; *photo*, 81
Boys from Syracuse, The (Rodgers/Hart), 13
Boys in the Band, The (Crowley), 45
Brando, Marlon, 16–17; *photo*, 8
Bread and Puppet Theatre, 102, 108, 113
Brecht, Bertolt, 53, 119; Off-Broadway, 39, 40–41; in regional theatre, 61, 73, 78, 80, 176, 177
Brig, The (Brown), 42
Brigadoon (Lerner/Loewe), 15
Broadway: actors, 16–17, 171; directors, 17–18, 143–44; dominance in 1950, 1–4, 11,22,56, 143–45; dramatists, 4–9, 80, 145–57, 169–71; economics, 19, 76, 90, 163–71, 176; and Lincoln Center, 70, 73, 75; musicals, 9–15, 17, 157–63; and Off-Broadway, 24–25, 39, 49, 53–54, 124–26, 171–72, 177; and Off Off-Broadway, 98, 116–19, 123–26, 171–72, 177; pre-Broadway tryouts, 19, 22, 56, 70, 175, 179; producers, 18–20, 26, 144; and regional theatre, 77, 79–83, 93, 171–72, 175, 177–84; road companies, 11, 22, 55, 175; role in 1950 and 1980 compared, 1–4, 22, 56, 171–72, 177–84; statistics, 163–71; status in 1980, 171–72, 175–84.
Brook, Peter, 120
Brown, Kenneth, 42
Browne, Roscoe Lee, 38; *photo*, 47
Brustein, Robert: quoted on Inge, 153; quoted on Living Theatre, 109, 111; quoted on Off-Broadway, 39, 53; quoted on O'Horgan, 112, 116
Brynner, Yul, 171
Bubbling Brown Sugar (various), 160
Bullins, Ed, 141
Buried Child (Shepard), 104, 131, 177; *photo*, 132
Burton, Richard, 159
Bus Stop (Inge), 144, 153
But For Whom Charlie (Behrman), 73, 75

Caffe Cino, 95–96, 97, 98, 100, 127, 131, 140
Cafe La Mama. *See* La Mama

California Suite (Simon), 70
Calm Down Mother (Terry), 141
Cambridge Ensemble, 103
Camelot (Lerner/Loewe), 159
Camino Real (Williams), 148
Candida (Shaw), 16
Caravan Theatre, 103
Carmines, Al, 99
Carousel (Rodgers/Hammerstein), 13
Cartier, Jacques, 63
Cat on a Hot Tin Roof (Williams), 144, 145–46, 147, 148
Caucasian Chalk Circle, The (Brecht), 73, 80
Center Stage, 88
Center Theatre Group, 88, 89, 127, 179; beginnings, 66–70, 85; compared to Repertory Theater of Lincoln Center, 74–76. *See also* Mark Taper Forum
Ceremonies in Dark Old Men (Elder), 51
Chaikin, Joseph, 101, 113
Chairs, The (Ionesco), 40
Champion, Gower, 144
Changeling, The (Middleton), 73
Changing Room, The (Storey), 80, 90
Changing Scene, 105
Channing, Carol, 171
Channing, Stockard, 103
Chapman, John: quoted on role of Broadway, 143; quoted on 1950 season, 165
Chapter Two (Simon), 156
Charles Playhouse, 61, 76, 103
Charley's Aunt (Thomas), 78
Chase, Mary Ellen, 9
Chayefsky, Paddy, 80, 154
Chekhov, Anton, 39, 56, 58, 78, 176
Chelsea Theater Center, 123, 124
Cherry Lane Theatre, 27
Chicago Alliance for the Performing Arts, 104
Children of a Lesser God (Medoff), 177; *photo*, 178
Chorus Line, A (Hamlisch/Kleban), 121, 161, 163; *photo*, 162–63; supports New York Shakespeare Festival, 124, 125, 181
Cino, Joseph, 95–96, 98; *photo*, 96
Circle in the Square, 41, 75, 96, 103, 180; beginnings, 27–31; continued strength, 46, 49, 124–25
Circle Repertory Company, 123, 124, 125, 127, 131, 136; *photos*, 134, 135

Circle Stage Company, 102
Civic Light Opera Company, 55, 66
Civic Repertory Theatre, 23
Clark, Bryan: *photo*, 106
Cleveland Play House, 21, 61, 80
Clift, Montgomery, 35
Clothes for a Summer Hotel (Williams), 149
Clurman, Harold: as director, 17–18, 20, 24, 28, 143; at Lincoln Center, 70, 73; quoted on Miller, 5; quoted on Williams, 6, 148
Cobb, Lee J., 17
Coburn, D. L., 82
Cocktail Party, The (Eliot), 22, 55
Cocteau, Jean, 33
Cohan, George M., 10
Cohen, Alexander, 144
Come Back, Little Sheba (Inge), 9, 56, 153
Come Blow Your Horn (Simon), 155
Comedians (Griffiths), 176
Commune (Performance Group), 113
Community Players (Houston), 57, 59
Community Players (Ojai), 57
Community theatre, 20–21, 57
Company (Sondheim), 161; *photo*, 164
Company Theatre, 115
Concept musical, 160
Condemned of Altona, The (Sartre), 73
Congreve, William, 78
Connecticut Yankee, A (Rodgers/Hart), 13
Connection, The (Gelber), 41–42, 111, 115
Cook, Ralph: quoted on Theatre Genesis, 99
Cornell, Katharine, 17, 22
Corn is Green, The (E. Williams), 22
Country Girl, The (Odets), 9
Country Playhouse, 56
Country Wife, The (Wycherley), 73
Coward, Noel, 176, 177
Cowboy Mouth (Shepard), 127, 129
Cowboys (Shepard), 98
Crawford, Cheryl, 24
Creation of the World and Other Business, The (Miller), 152
Creditors (Strindberg), 22
Crescent Theatre, 24
Cristofer, Michael, 80, 157, 181
Cronyn, Hume, 62, 79; *photo*, 82
Crouse, Russel, 9
Crowley, Mart, 45

Crucible, The (Miller), 149
CSC Repertory Company, 102
Cunningham, Merce: *photo*, 34

Dallas Theater Center, 63, 80, 86
Dames at Sea (Wise/Haimsohn/
    Miller), 95
Dancin' (various), 160
D'Angelo, Aristide, 15
Danner, Blythe, 103
Danton's Death (Büchner), 73
Dark at the Top of the Stairs, The (Inge),
    58, 153
Davidson, Gordon, 66–70; *photo*, 67;
    quoted on transfers to Broadway,
    181, 182
Day of Absence (Ward), 52
DC Black Repertory Theater, 103
Death of a Salesman (Miller), 5–6, 17,
    22, 143, 144, 149, 151
Death of Bessie Smith, The (Albee), 42
Delacorte, George, 38
Delacorte Theater, 38, 50, 51, 87;
    photo, 50. *See also* New York Shake-
    speare Festival
Delicate Balance, A (Albee), 45, 154
DeMille, Agnes, 12
DeNiro, Robert, 98
Dennis, Sandy, 171
Desert Song, The (Romberg/Hammer-
    stein), 13
Detective Story (Kingsley), 9, 22, 143
Devils, The (Whiting), 68
Dewhurst, Colleen, 38, 70
Diary of Ann Frank, The (Goodrich/
    Hackett), 144
Dillman, Bradford: *photo*, 32
Dionysus in 69 (Performance Group),
    112, 114, 115
Doctor Faustus Lights the Lights
    (Stein), 33
Dorothy Chandler Pavilion, 66;
    photo, 68
Douglas, Kirk, 171
Drake, Alfred, 17, 171
Drama Review, The, 101
Dramatic Mirror, The, 10-11
Dream Play (Pageant Players), 115
Duck Variations, The (Mamet), 136
Dunaway, Faye, 40
Durang, Christopher, 80
Dutchman (Jones), 45
Duvall, Robert, 103

East-West Players, 104
Eccentricities of a Nightingale (Wil-
    liams), 146
*Effect of Gamma Rays on Man-in-the-
    Moon Marigolds, The* (Zindel), 83
Egan, Jenny: *photo*, 81
Eichelberger, James: *photo*, 130
Eikenberry, Jill: *photo*, 106
Elder, Lonnie, 51
Eldridge, Florence, 17; *photo*, 32
Elephant Man, The (Pomerance), 90,
    175
Eliot, T. S., 22, 33
Elitch Gardens, 55
El Teatro Campesino, 105
Empty Space Theatre, 105
Endgame (Beckett), 40, 46
Enemy of the People, An (Ibsen/Miller),
    149, 176
Engel, Lehman, 160
Eugene O'Neill Theater Center, 105,
    127, 177; *photo*, 106
Evanston Theatre Company, 104
Experimental theatre, 31–33, 101–2,
    104, 108–21. *See also* Alternative
    theatre; Improvisation
Eyen, Tom, 98, 100, 140

False Promises (S.F. Mime Troupe):
    photo, 107
Fanny (Rome), 144
Fantasticks, The (Jones/Schmidt), 25,
    48
Fascinating Flora (Kerker), 10–11
Federal Theatre, 23
Feiffer, Jules, 49
Feldman, Peter: *photo*, 34
Ferrell, Conchata: *photo*, 134
Ferrer, José, 20
Fichandler, Zelda, 60, 78; *photo*, 60
Fiddler on the Roof (Bock/Harnick),
    144, 159, 167
Fifth of July (Wilson), 135; *photo*, 135
Finian's Rainbow (Lane/Harburg), 13
Firehouse Theater, 103–4, 112, 127
First Stone, The (Ferris), 165
Florida Studio Theatre, 105
Flower Drum Song (Rodgers/
    Hammerstein), 157–58
Folger Theatre Group, 103
Follies (Sondheim), 162
Fontaine, Lynn, 17, 22
*For Colored Girls Who Have Considered
    Suicide . . .* (Shange), 126, 183

Ford Foundation, 80, 86, 87–89, 91–92, 126
Fosse, Bob, 160
Foster, Paul, 115
Fourteen Hundred Thousand (Shepard), 129
4th Street Theatre, 39
Foxworth, Robert, 79
Frankel, Gene, 46
Frankenstein (Living Theatre), 108, 114
Fred Miller Theatre, 61, 88. *See also* Milwaukee Repertory Theater Company
Freedman, Gerald, 48
Freeman, David, 106
Free Southern Theater, 89, 105
Frelich, Phyllis: *photo,* 178
Friml, Rudolf, 10, 13
Front Street Theatre, 61, 76
Funny Thing Happened on the Way to the Forum, A (Sondheim), 160
Furth, George, 161
Futz (Owens), 116

Gallows Humor (Richardson), 46
Garfield, David, 16, 17; quoted on method acting, 16
Garrick Gaities, The (Rodgers/ Hart), 13
Garson, Barbara, 52
Gazzara, Ben, 40
Gelber, Jack, 41–42, 49; *photo,* 34
Genêt, Jean, 41, 46
Gentlemen Prefer Blondes (Styne/ Robin), 22
George Street Playhouse, 177
Gershwin, George, 11
Gershwin, Ira, 11, 12
Gilman, Richard: quoted on Living Theatre, 120
Gin Game, The (Coburn): *photo,* 82
Gingerbread Lady, The (Simon), 156
Glass Menagerie, The (Williams), 6–7, 143, 147–48
Glore, John: quoted on Seattle Rep, 63
Godspell (Schwartz), 48
Gogol, Nikolai, 24, 78
Goin' a Buffalo (Bullins), 141
Golden Apple, The (Latouche/ Moross), 48
Goldman, Donald, 39
Goldman, William: quoted on Simon, 156
Goldoni, Carlo, 176

Goodbye Girl, The (Simon), 156
Goodman Theatre, 61, 80, 83, 104; *photo,* 137
Goodspeed Opera House, 179
Good Woman of Setzuan, The (Brecht), 41
Gordon, Max, 20
Gordone, Charles, 51
Gottfried, Martin: quoted on dangers of subsidy, 91; quoted on regional theatres and Broadway, 179, 180
Grease (Jacobs/Casey), 161, 163, 169, 177
Great White Hope, The (Sackler), 83, 90, 171; *photo,* 84
Gregory, André, 65, 102, 113; quoted on Theatre of the Living Arts, 65
Grey, Joel, 40, 171
Griffith, Trevor, 176
Grimes, Tammy, 40, 171
Grizzard, George, 79
Grotowski, Jerzy, 119
Group Theatre, 15, 17, 24
Guare, John, 70, 105, 176
Guernsey, Otis L., Jr.: quoted on Broadway, 165, 171-72; quoted on David Merrick, 144; quoted on musicals, 159, 160; quoted on Off-Broadway, 53
Guggenheim Foundation, 126
Guthrie, Tyrone, 61–62; *photo,* 62
Guys and Dolls (Loesser), 15, 55
Gypsy (Styne/Sondheim), 159

Hailey, Oliver, 70, 80
Hair (Ragni/Rado/MacDermot), 51, 53, 125, 167, 169, 171, 181; *photo,* 118; staging effects, 116–19, 161
Hairy Ape, The (O'Neill), 30
Hall, Ed: *photo,* 130
Hambleton, T. Edward, 35; *photo,* 36
Hammerstein, Oscar II, 11, 20, 159, 161, 162; plays analyzed, 12–13, 157–58
Handke, Peter, 176
Hansberry, Lorraine, 154
Happy Days (Beckett), 40
Harburg, E. Y., 13
Harris, Cynthia: *photo,* 182
Harris, Julie, 17
Harrison, Rex, 158
Harry, Noon and Night (Ribman), 46
Hartford Stage Company, 63, 80, 86, 88
Hart, Lorenz, 11, 12, 13

Hart, Moss, 176
Harvey (Chase), 9
Hayes, Helen, 17
Heggen, Thomas, 9
Heiress, The (Goetz), 56
Helen G. Bonfils Theatre, 176
Hellman, Lillian, 9, 169, 176
Hello, Dolly! (Herman), 144, 154, 160, 168
Henie, Sonia, 20
Hepburn, Katharine, 22
Herbert, F. Hugh, 154
Herbert, Victor, 10
Herne, James A., 4
Heston, Charlton, 171
Hewes, Henry: quoted on 1962 Broadway season, 165
Hirsch, Judd, 40, 98
History of the American Film, A (Durang), 80
Hoffman, Dustin, 40, 103
Hogan, Jonathan: *photo*, 135
Hogan's Goat (Alfred), 46
Holbrook, Hal, 40, 70
Home of the Brave (Laurents), 9
Hooks, Robert, 52
Horovitz, Israel, 70, 100, 105, 140, 176
Hotchkiss, Marlow: quoted on Firehouse Theater, 103
Hot l Baltimore, The (Wilson), 90, 123, 125, 133; *photo*, 134
Houghton, Norris, 35; *photo*, 36
Houseman, John, 66
House of Blue Leaves (Guare), 105
Hub Theatre Centre, 103
Hudson Guild, 123
Huffman, David: *photo*, 182
Hughie (O'Neill), 154
Hurt, William, 40
Huston, Walter, 159

Ibsen, Henrik, 5, 58, 78, 149, 176
Icarus's Mother (Shepard), 98, 127
Iceman Cometh, The (O'Neill), 7, 30, 154
I Know My Love (Behrman), 22
Improvisation, 41, 46, 104, 112–13, 115, 121, 141
Incident at Vichy (Miller), 73, 151
Indiana Repertory Theatre, 78
Indians (Kopit), 79, 80
Indian Wants the Bronx, The (Horovitz), 105, 140
Inge, William, 9, 58, 149, 153, 169
Inherit the Wind (Lawrence/Lee), 80

Inner City Repertory Company, 65–66, 78, 89
In New England Winter (Bullins), 141
Inspector General, The (Gogol), 78
Interplayers, 26
In the Bar of a Tokyo Hotel (Williams), 148
In the Boom Boom Room (Rabe), 137-38
In the Jungle of Cities (Brecht), 41
In the Matter of J. Robert Oppenheimer (Kipphardt), 68
In the Wine Time (Bullins), 141
In White America (Duberman), 105
Ionesco, Eugene, 40, 42, 43, 53
Iowa Theatre Lab, 105
Irene (Tierney/McCarthy), 171
Irish Players, 39
Irving, Jules, 61, 73, 75, 76

James Joyce Memorial Liquid Theatre, The (Company Theatre), 115
JB (MacLeish), 154
Jellicoe, Ann, 103
Jesse and the Bandit Queen (Freeman): *photo*, 106
Jesus Christ Superstar (Webber/Rice), 119
John Loves Mary (Krasna), 9, 56
Johns, Glynis, 159
Jones, James Earl, 38, 51; *photo*, 84
Jones, LeRoi, 45, 49, 51
Jones, Margo, 57–59, 76, 77; *photo*, 57; quoted on regional theatre, 57
Jones, Preston, 80
Jones, Tom, 48, 49
Jonson, Ben, 78
Jory, Jon, 65
Joseph Jefferson Theatre Company, 102
Journey of the Fifth Horse, The (Ribman), 46
Joyce, Stephen, 79
Judson Memorial Church, 99
Judson Poets' Theatre, 99, 123
Julia, Raul, 124
Julian Theatre, 104
Juilliard School of Music, 70; *photo*, 71

Kanin, Garson, 9, 169
Kauffmann, Stanley: quoted on Simon, 157; quoted on Williams, 147
Kaufman, George S., 176
Kazan, Elia: as director, 17–18, 20, 24, 28, 143; at Lincoln Center, 70,

73, 75; *photo*, 18; quoted on method acting, 16
Keach, Stacy, 40, 79
Keep Tightly Closed in a Cool Dry Place (Terry), 141
Kennedy, Adrienne, 70
Kennedy Center, 83
Kennedy's Children (Patrick), 96, 140–41
Kern, Jerome, 10, 11, 12, 13, 48
Kerr, Deborah, 171
Kerr, Walter: quoted on Living Theatre, 111; quoted on Simon, 156
Kert, Larry: *photo*, 164
King and I, The (Rodgers/Hammerstein), 157
King of Schnorrers (Woldin), 177
Kingsley, Sidney, 4, 9, 24, 169
Kingston Mines Theatre, 177
Kipphardt, Heiner, 68
Kiss Me Kate (Porter), 15, 22
Kleiman, Harlan, 65
Knack, The (Jellicoe), 103
Kneeland, Richard: *photo*, 44
Knickerbocker Holiday (Weill/Anderson), 159
Kopit, Arthur, 46, 53, 79, 80, 83
Krapp's Last Tape (Beckett), 40
Krasna, Norman, 9
Kronenberger, Louis: quoted on 1956 Broadway season, 165; quoted on Williams, 147

Lady from Dubuque, The (Albee), 155
Lady in the Dark (Weill/Gershwin), 12
Lafayette Theatre, 24
La Jolla Playhouse, 55
La Mama, 89, 98, 100–101, 115, 116, 123, 124, 126, 127
La Mama Hollywood, 104
Lane, Burton, 13
Langella, Frank, 40, 79; *photo*, 47
Langley, Stephen: quoted on regional theatre, 59, 184
Lansky, Zane: *photo*, 134
Last Meeting of the Knights of the White Magnolia, The (P. Jones), 80
Last of the Red Hot Lovers (Simon), 155, 156
Latent Heterosexual, The (Chayefsky), 80
Laurents, Arthur, 9, 159
Lawrence, Jerome, 80
League of New York Theatres, 169

League of Resident Theatres, 77
Leave It to Jane (Kern/Bolton/Wodehouse), 48
Lee, Robert E., 80
LeGallienne, Eva, 22, 23
Lemmon, Jack, 171
Lemon Sky (Wilson), 105
Lenny (Barry), 119
Lenya, Lotte, 39
Lerner, Alan Jay, 11, 15, 158-59, 169; quoted on *My Fair Lady*, 158
Lesson, The (Ionesco), 40
Libin, Paul, 179
Life in the Theatre, A (Mamet), 80, 136–37; *photo*, 137
Life with Father (Lindsay/Crouse), 9
Lincoln Center for the Performing Arts, 70, 75, 83, 85, 125; *photo*, 71. *See also* Repertory Theater of Lincoln Center; Vivian Beaumont Theater
Lincoln Theatre, 24
Lindsay, Howard, 9
Line (Horovitz), 140
Little, Stuart W.: quoted on Albee, 45; quoted on Phoenix Theatre, 37
Little Mary Sunshine (Besoyan), 48
Little Murders (Feiffer), 49
Little Night Music, A (Sondheim), 159, 162
Live Like Pigs (Arden), 103
Living Theatre, 49; beginnings, 27, 31–35, 97; and *The Connection*, 41–42; exile, 42, 49; return tour, 52, 108–11; its significance, 112–21
Loesser, Frank, 15, 159
Loewe, Frederick, 11, 15, 158-59
Logan, Joshua, 9, 11, 18, 144
Long Day's Journey into Night (O'Neill), 7, 29, 31, 152, 154; *photo*, 32
Long Wharf Theatre, 63, 80, 83, 86; *photos*, 82, 139
Look Back in Anger (Osborne), 40, 144
Loose Ends (Weller), 177
Loretto-Hilton Center, 63, 86
Los Angeles Actors' Theatre, 104
Los Angeles Philharmonic, 66
Lovers and Enemies (Artzybashell), 165
Lowell, Robert, 46
Lu Ann Hampton Laverty Oberlander (P. Jones), 80
Luckinbill, Laurence: *photo*, 182
Lunt, Alfred, 17, 22

Macbeth (Shakespeare), 78
MacBird! (Garson), 52
McCarter Theatre, 63
McGill, Bruce: *photo*, 130
MacLeish, Archibald, 154
McNally, Terrence, 70, 80, 140
Mad Dog Blues (Shepard), 129, 131
Madness of Lady Bright, The (Wilson), 98, 131
Magic Theatre, 104, 127; *photo*, 132
Malina, Judith, 31–35, 41–42, 108–12; *photo*, 34
Mame Herman), 80, 160
Mamet, David, 80, 83, 104, 127, 141, 157, 176, 177; plays analyzed, 136–37
Manhattan Project, 102, 113, 125
Manhattan Theatre Club, 123, 125
Mann, Theodore, 27, 46, 125
Man of La Mancha (Leigh/Darion), 159
Mantle, Burns: quoted on 1927 Broadway season, 165
Many Loves (W. C. Williams), 41, 42
Marat/Sade (Weiss), 120, 144
March, Frederick, 17; *photo*, 32
Marco Millions (O'Neill), 73
Mark Taper Forum, 66, 74, 77, 80, 86, 87, 177; *photos*, 68, 69, 178, 182. *See also* Center Theatre Group
Marlin-Jones, Davey: quoted on Washington Theater Club, 102, 103
Marlowe, Christopher, 78
Martin, Mary, 17; *photo*, 14
Mason, Marshall W., 98, 101, 123; *photo*, 122
Matchmaker, The (Wilder), 154
Me and Juliet (Rodgers/Hammerstein), 157
Mednick, Murray, 99
Medoff, Mark, 123, 157, 177
Meeker, Ralph, 70
Meisner, Sanford, 15
Melfi, Leonard, 70, 99, 100, 140
Member of the Wedding, The (McCullers), 17, 22
Memory of Two Mondays, A (Miller), 151
Merchant of Venice, The (Shakespeare), 51
Merman, Ethel, 17, 159
Merrick, David, 144, 168
Method acting, 15–17
Metropolitan Opera House, 70, 75; *photo*, 71

Middleton, Thomas, 73
Mielziner, Jo, 17
Miller, Arthur, 9, 59, 78, 143, 169, 176; at Lincoln Center, 70, 73, 75; *photo*, 150; plays analyzed, 4–6, 149–52
Miller, Jason, 126, 157
Milwaukee Repertory Theater Company, 61, 83, 85, 89. *See also* Fred Miller Theatre
Minskoff Theatre, 125
Misfits, The (Miller), 151
Miss Margarida's Way (Athayde), 183
Missouri Repertory Theatre, 87
Mister Roberts (Logan/Heggen), 9, 22
Molière, 65, 73, 176
Monroe, Marilyn, 151
Montserrat (Hellman), 9
Moon for the Misbegotten, A (O'Neill), 7, 30, 49
Moon is Blue, The (Herbert), 154
Moore, Edward J., 123
More Stately Mansions (O'Neill), 70, 154
Moriarty, Michael, 40
Moscow Art Theatre, 15, 24
Most Happy Fella, The (Loesser), 159
Motel (van Itallie), 141
Mound Builders, The (Wilson), 123, 133–35
Mousetrap, The (Christie), 176
Mummers, 60–61, 83; causes of failure, 86, 91; and Ford Foundation, 86, 87, 88, 89
Murderous Angels (O'Brien), 70
Musicals: beginnings, 9–10; concept musical, 160–63; conventions, 10–13; maturity, 12–15, 157–59; Off-Broadway, 39, 48; Off Off-Broadway, 99, 102; performers, 17, 158–59; stagnation, 159–60
Music Center of the County of Los Angeles, 66, 83; *photo*, 68. *See also* Center Theatre Group; Mark Taper Forum
Music Man, The (Willson), 144, 159, 175, 176
My Fair Lady (Lerner/Loewe), 11, 12, 158–59
Mysteries and Other Pieces (Living Theatre), 108, 113

National Council on the Arts, 144
National Endowment for the Arts, 66, 77, 90, 126, 177, 184

National Playwrights Conference, 105

National Theatre of the Deaf, 105

Nederlander, James M.: quoted on pre-Broadway tryouts, 179–80

Needles, William: *photo,* 81

Negro Ensemble Company, 52, 89

New Federal Theatre, 125

New Lafayette Theater, 52

Newman, Danny, 92

New Mexico State University, 177

New Playwrights' Theatre of Washington, 103

New Theatre for Now, 70, 74, 89

New York City Ballet, 70

New York City Opera, 70

New York Philharmonic, 70

New York Public Library, 70

New York Shakespeare Festival, 100, 124; beginnings, 27, 37–39, 40, 48; funding, 51, 88, 90, 124, 181; at Lincoln Center, 74, 75, 76; new plays, 51, 117, 125–26, 137, 157, 183; on, Off- and Off Off-Broadway, 51, 53, 117, 124, 125–26, 171, 181, 183

New York State Council on the Arts, 90, 126

New York State Theater: *photo,* 71

New York Times, 62, 168

Next (McNally), 140

Nichols, Mike, 144

Night of the Iguana, The (Williams), 146, 148

Night Thoreau Spent in Jail, The (Lawrence/Lee), 80

1940's Radio Hour, The (W. Jones), 177

Nolte, Nick, 98

No, No, Nanette (Youmans/Harbach/Caesar), 171

No Place To Be Somebody (Gordone), 51

Norman Conquests, The (Ayckbourn), 70

North Light Repertory Company, 104

Nussbaum, Michael: *photo,* 137

O'Brien, Conor Cruise, 70

Octagon Theatre, 102

Odd Couple, The (Simon), 156

Odets, Clifford, 4, 5, 9, 24

Odyssey Theatre Ensemble, 104

Off-Broadway: actors, 29–30, 35, 38, 40, 51; beginnings, 21–27; and Broadway, 24–25, 39, 49, 53–54, 124–26, 171–72, 177; directors, 28–31, 40, 41–42, 46–48; dramatists, 40–46, 49; economics, 27, 49, 52–53, 88, 89; middle period, 40–48; and Off Off-Broadway, 96–97, 98, 124–26; and regional theatre, 53–54, 75, 79, 83, 102, 103; significance, 24–25, 29; third period, 48–54, 175

Off-Broadway Incorporated, 26

Off-Broadway Theatre League, 26

Office of Juvenile Delinquency, 99

Off Off-Broadway: actors, 98; beginnings, 25, 52, 95–102; and Broadway, 98, 116–19, 123–26, 171–72, 177; directors, 98, 101; dramatists, 97, 100, 123, 126–42; history, 121–26, 175; and Off-Broadway, 96–97, 98, 124–26; and regional theatre, 98, 102, 103; and subsidy, 89, 91, 99

Oh Dad Poor Dad . . . (Kopit), 46

O'Horgan, Tom, 98, 112, 115; directorial style, 101, 116–19; influence, 121, 161

Oklahoma! (Rodgers/Hammerstein), 12–13, 20, 22

Oldest Living Graduate, The (P. Jones), 80

Old Glory, The (Lowell), 46; *photo,* 47

Oliver (Bart), 144

Omaha Magic Theatre, 105

Once Upon a Mattress (M. Rodgers/Barer), 48

O'Neill, Eugene, 4, 7, 24, 29, 152; *photo,* 30; posthumous rediscovery, 30–31, 70, 154–55; widely produced, 49, 59, 73, 78, 176

O'Neill Center. See Eugene O'Neill Theatre Center

Open Theatre, 100, 101, 112-13, 120, 126, 141

Operation Sidewinder (Shepard), 128

Organic Theater Company, 104

Osborne, John, 40, 144

Othello (Shakespeare), 51

Out Cry (Williams), 148

Owens, Rochelle, 65, 116, 127

Pacific Overtures (Sondheim), 162

Pacino, Al, 17, 40, 98, 103, 171

Page, Geraldine, 17, 29

Pageant Players, 113, 115

Pajama Game (Adler/Ross), 144

Palance, Jack, 40

Pal Joey (Rodgers/Hart), 12, 13

Papp, Joseph: described, 37, 100; founds New York Shakespeare Festival, 37–38, 48, 51; at Lincoln Center, 74, 75, 76; *photo*, 38; quoted on acting, 27; quoted on new audiences, 37; quoted on using Broadway, 181; uses Broadway, 125–26, 180, 181, 183

Paradise Now (Living Theatre), 108, 111, 114, 115; *photo*, 110

Pasadena Community Playhouse, 21, 57

Patrick, John, 154

Patrick, Robert, 70, 96, 140

Patton, Lucille: *photo*, 81

People's Drama, 26

People's Theatre, 103

Perelman, S. J., 169

Performance Community, 104

Performance Group, 101, 112, 113, 114, 123

Performing Arts Center (Milwaukee), 85

Peters, Bernadette, 98

Phoenix Theatre, 40, 41, 46, 48, 65, 88; and APA, 49, 53, 171; beginnings, 26, 35–37

Picasso, Pablo, 33

Picnic (Inge), 153

Pinero, Miguel, 125

Pinter, Harold, 53, 61, 78

Pinza, Ezio: *photo*, 14

Pipe Dream (Rodgers/Hammerstein), 157

Pippin (Schwartz), 169

Pirandello, Luigi, 41, 65, 78

Pirates of Penzance, The (Gilbert/Sullivan), 181

Piscator, Erwin, 119

Pittsburgh Playhouse, 65, 75, 76, 78

Players Theatre of Boston, 103

Playgroup Inc., 105

Plays in Progress, 89

Playwrights' Company, 20

Playwrights Horizons, 123

Playwright's Lab, 177

Playwrights Unit, 45, 70, 102

Plaza Suite (Simon), 144

Porgy (Hayward), 165

Porter, Cole, 11, 15

Pound, Ezra, 33

Preston, Robert, 159

Price, The (Miller), 144, 152

Primary English Class, The (Horovitz), 140

Prince, Harold, 121, 144, 161, 162; *photo*, 166

Princeton University, 63

Private Lives (Coward), 22

Prodigal, The (Richardson), 46

Provincetown Playhouse, 23–24, 27

Public Theater, 51, 76, 117, 125, 181. *See also* New York Shakespeare Festival

Pulitzer Prize, 51, 97, 104, 171, 177, 181

Pygmalion (Shaw), 158

Quintero, José, 27–31, 40, 46, 53, 70, 73; *photo*, 28

Rabb, Ellis, 35, 63

Rabe, David, 83, 126, 136, 137–38, 157; quoted on *Sticks and Bones*, 138

Raisin (Woldin/Brittan), 83

Raisin in the Sun, A (Hansberry), 154

Rea, Oliver, 62

Reality Theatre, 103

Red Cross (Shepard), 129

Reehling, Joyce: *photo*, 135

Reeve, Christopher, 40

Repertory Theatre New Orleans, 65–66, 76, 91

Regional theatre: actors, 79; artistic interference, 65, 73, 78, 91–92; audiences, 63, 74–76, 77, 78–79; beginnings, 57–66; and Broadway, 70, 73, 75, 77, 79–83, 93, 171–72, 175, 177–84; dramatists, 68–69, 78, 80–83, 126–27; economics, 73, 76, 87–93; failures, 65, 66, 70–76, 86; and Off-Broadway, 75, 79, 83, 102, 103; and Off Off-Broadway, 98, 102, 103; organization and repertory, 58, 77–79, 175–77; subsidy, 58, 83, 86, 87–93, 184–85; theatre buildings, 83–87, 89, 176

Repertory Theater of Lincoln Center, 66, 70–76, 86, 87, 144, 151

Resident theatre. *See* Regional theatre

Respectful Prostitute, The (Sartre), 22

Ribman, Ronald, 46

Richardson, Jack, 46

Ridiculous Theatrical Company, 102

Ritz, The (McNally), 140

Riverside Church, 99, 125

Road companies, 11, 22, 55, 175

Robards, Jason, Jr., 30, 70; *photo*, 32

Robbins, Jerome, 160; *photo,* 36
Rockefeller Brothers Fund, 88, 89, 90
Rockefeller Foundation, 89, 126
Rodgers, Richard, 11, 20, 159, 161, 169; plays analyzed, 12–13, 157–58
Romberg, Sigmund, 10, 13
Room Service (Murray/Boretz), 65
Rose Marie (Friml/Hammerstein), 13
Rose Tattoo, The (Williams), 148
Ross, David, 39
Rothchilds, The (Bock/Harnick), 167
Royal Shakespeare Company, 120
Rubenstein, John: *photo,* 178
Rudkin, David, 80, 125
Runaways (Swados), 183

Sackler, Howard, 83
Sainer, Arthur: quoted on experimental theatre, 113–14, 115–16
Saint Clements Church, 99
Saint Joan (Shaw), 73
Saint Mark's-in-the-Bouwerie, 99
Sandbox, The (Albee), 42
San Francisco Mime Troupe, 104, 108; *photo,* 107
Sankey, Tom, 99
Sartre, Jean-Paul, 22, 73
Schechner, Richard, 101
Schisgal, Murray, 46, 49, 53
Schmidt, Harvey, 48, 49
Schneider, Alan, 46, 53, 79–80, 144
Schwartz, Maurice, 23
Scism, Mack, 60
Scott, George C., 38, 51
Sea Horse, The (Moore), 123
Seattle Repertory Theatre, 63–65, 78, 88
Seesaw (Coleman/Fields), 167
Serpent, The (van Itallie), 113, 141
Sexual Perversity in Chicago (Mamet), 104, 136
Shadow Box, The (Cristofer), 80, 90, 157, 181–83; *photo,* 182
Shakespeare, William: on Broadway, 22, 93; Off-Broadway, 24, 37–39, 51; in regional theatre, 56, 58, 65, 78, 93, 103, 176
Shakespeare Workshop, 37
Shakespearewrights, 39
Shange, Ntozake, 126, 183
Shaved Splits (Shepard), 131
Shaw, George Bernard, 11, 73, 78, 158
Shaw, Irwin, 169
Sheldon, Edward, 4
Shenar, Paul: *photo,* 64

Shepard, Sam: influences, 120, 121; and Off Off-Broadway, 97, 98, 99, 100, 127; *photo,* 128; plays analyzed, 127–31; and regional theatre, 80, 104, 127, 176, 177
Short Eyes (Pinero), 125
Show Boat (Kern/Hammerstein), 12, 13, 165
Showcases, 21–22, 26, 97, 104, 121–23
Shubert Organization, 20
Simon, Neil, 70, 78, 171, 176, 179; plays analyzed, 155–57
Skinner, Margo: *photo,* 44
Small Craft Warnings (Williams), 148
Smith, Cecil: quoted on Cohan, 10; quoted on *Oklahoma!,* 12
Smith, Michael: quoted on Off Off-Broadway, 97
Solitaire/Double Solitaire (Anderson), 80
So Long at the Fair (Wilson), 97
Sondheim, Stephen, 144, 159, 171; *photo,* 166; plays analyzed, 161–63; quoted on musicals, 159, 161
Sorvino, Paul, 124
Sound of Music, The (Rodgers/Hammerstein), 158
South Pacific (Rodgers/Hammerstein), 11, 13, 22, 157; *photo,* 14
Spicer, James: *photo,* 34
Stage/West, 88
Stanislavski, Konstantin, 15–16, 24
Stanley, Kim, 17, 40
Stein, Gertrude, 33, 99
Stevens, Roger L., 144
Stewart, Ellen, 100; *photo,* 101
Sticks and Bones (Rabe), 126, 137, 138, 171, 183
Stoppard, Tom, 176
Storey, David, 80
Strange Interlude (O'Neill), 30, 165
Strasberg, Lee, 15–16, 24
Streamers (Rabe), 83, 137, 138; *photo,* 139
Streep, Meryl, 40
Streetcar Named Desire, A (Williams), 7, 16–17, 22, 145, 146, 147, 148; *photo,* 8
Street theatre, 102, 104, 108, 112, 113; *photo,* 107
Strindberg, August, 22, 24
Studio Arena Theatre, 61, 78, 80, 86, 127; *photo,* 81
Studio Seven, 26
Styne, Jule, 159

Subsidy: dangers, 86, 91–92, 184; by foundations, 83, 87–91, 126; by government, 23, 65–66, 90, 99, 126, 184; significance, 92–93, 184–85. *See also* Regional theatre, artistic interference
Suddenly Last Summer Williams), 147
Summer and Smoke (Williams), 21, 28, 29, 58, 146, 148
Summer Stock, 21, 55–56
Sunshine Boys, The (Simon), 155–56
Swados, Elizabeth, 121
Sweeney Todd (Sondheim), 90, 163
Sweet Bird of Youth (Williams), 146, 147
Syndicate, 3
Syracuse Repertory Theatre, 63

Theatre '47, 21, 57–59, 77
Theatre Genesis, 98, 99
Theatre Group. *See* Center Theatre Group
Theatre Guild, 19, 20, 24, 56
Theatre-in-the-Round (M. Jones), 57–58
Theatre of the Living Arts, 65, 76, 78
Theatre Workshop Boston, 103
Theatre X, 105
Theme musical, 160
They're Playing Our Song (Hamlisch/ Singer), 156, 175
Thirkield, Rob, 123
Thomashevsky, Boris, 23
Threepenny Opera, The (Weill/Brecht), 25, 39, 40, 48
Tiger, The (Schisgal), 46
Time of Your Life, The (Saroyan), 65
Tiny Alice (Albee), 45, 155
TKTS Discount Ticket Booth, 90, 169; *photo*, 170
Todd, Michael, 20
Tom Paine (Foster), 115
Tone, Franchot, 17
Talley's Folly (Wilson), 123, 135–36
Talmer, Jerry, 96
Tandy, Jessica, 62, 79; *photo, 8, 82*
Tartuffe (Molière), 73
Tea and Sympathy (Anderson), 154
Teahouse of the August Moon, The (J. Patrick), 154
Tiebele and her Demon (Singer/Friedman), 177
Tenth Man, The (Chayefsky), 154
Terry, Megan, 52, 100, 112, 141
"Texas Trilogy" (P. Jones), 80
That Lady (O'Brien), 22

That Championship Season (J. Miller), 90, 126, 157, 183
Theatre Atlanta, 61
Theatre Collective, 23
Theatre Communications Group, 89, 91–92, 126
Theatre Company of Boston, 103, 127
Theatre de Lys, 39
Theatre Development Fund, 90–91, 126, 169
Theatre for Tomorrow, 89
Tonight We Improvise (Pirandello), 41
Tony Award, 171, 177, 181
Tooth of Crime, The (Shepard), 129–31; *photo*, 130
Touch of the Poet, A (O'Neill), 154
Touliatos, George, 61
Trinity Square Repertory Company, 66, 88; *photos*, 44, 130
Trinity University, 63
Truckline Cafe (M. Anderson), 16
Twentieth Century Fund, 83, 85–86, 88, 90
Two Gentlemen of Verona (MacDermot/Guare), 125, 171, 181
Typists, The (Schisgal), 46
Tyrone Guthrie Theater, 79, 86, 88, 103, 177; beginnings, 61–63, 74, 85

University theatre, 20, 63, 66, 80
Unseen Hand, The Shepard), 131
Uris Theatre, 125

Vance, Nina, 59; *photo, 59*
van Itallie, Jean-Claude, 52, 113, 127, 141
Vaughan, Stuart, 40, 48, 65, 79
Via Galactica (MacDermot/Gore), 76
Victory at Sea (Rodgers), 157
Victory Gardens Theater, 104
Viet Rock (Terry), 52, 112, 141
View from the Bridge, A (Miller), 151
Village Voice, 96
Vivian Beaumont Theater, 70, 75, 86, 87; *photos*, 71, 72. *See also* Lincoln Center; Repertory Theater of Lincoln Center
Voight, Jon, 103

Waiting for Godot (Beckett), 40, 46, 105
Waller, Fats, 160
Ward, Douglas Turner, 52
Warp (St. Edmund/Gordon), 104
Washington Square Players, 23–24

Washington Theater Club, 102–3, 127

Water Engine, The (Mamet), 137

Wayne, David, 70

Weaver, Sigourney, 40

Webster, John, 49

Webster College, 63

Weill, Kurt, 12, 39

Welles, Orson, 176

We Present, 26

West Side Story (Bernstein/Sondheim), 144, 159, 160, 162

When You Comin' Back, Red Ryder? (Medoff), 123

Where's Charley? (Loesser), 22, 55

White, Cosmo: *photo,* 137

White, Jane, 124

White Devil, The (Webster), 49

Whitehead, Robert, 70, 73, 75, 144

White Whore and the Bit Player, The (Eyen), 98, 140

Whiting, John, 68

Who's Afraid of Virginia Woolf? (Albee), 43–45, 131, 155; *photo,* 44

Wilder, Clinton, 45, 70, 102

Wilder, Thornton, 4, 78, 154

Williams, Tennessee, 16, 28, 143, 169; influence, 9, 42, 149, 153; *photo,* 145; plays analyzed, 4, 6–7, 145–49, 152; quoted on himself, 149; quoted on Inge, 153; in regional theatres, 21, 58, 59, 78, 176, 177

Williams, William Carlos, 41

Wilson, John C., 20

Wilson, Lanford, 141, 157; and Circle Repertory Company, 123, 127, 131–33, 136; early experience, 70, 97, 98, 100–1, 105, 127; *photo,* 133; plays analyzed, 131–36; quoted on his plays, 131

Wings (Kopit), 83, 90

Wisdom Bridge Theatre, 104

Wiz, The (Smalls), 169

Woods, The (Mamet), 136

Words and Music, 104

Worker's Drama League, 23

Wycherley, William, 73

Yale Repertory Theatre, 63, 83, 86

Yale University, 63, 108, 111

Yama, Conrad: *photo,* 81

Yiddish theatre, 15, 23–24

You Know I Can't Hear You When the Water's Running (Anderson), 154

You're a Good Man, Charlie Brown (Gesner), 48

Your Own Thing (Hester/Apolinar), 48

Zeigler, Joseph Wesley; quoted on dangers of subsidy, 91–92; quoted on Lincoln Center, 73; quoted on regional theatre, 58, 62, 181, 183–84

Zeisler, Peter, 62

Zerbe, Anthony, 79

Ziegfield, Florenz, Jr., 10

Zindel, Paul, 83

Zoo Story, The (Albee), 42–43, 45